The Last Shepherd's Dog

and Other Stories From a Rural Spanish Village
High and Hidden in the Costa Blanca Mountains

John Sunderland

Copyright ©2017 by John Sunderland
All rights reserved.

No part of this publication may be reproduced, distributed, or transmitted in any form or by any means, including photocopying, recording, or other electronic or mechanical methods, without the prior written permission of the publisher, except as permitted by U.S. copyright law. For permission requests, contact info@johnsunderland.co.uk
Alternate contact: kathleenkirkpatrick@me.com

For privacy reasons, some names, locations, and dates may have been changed.

Cover and interior illustrations by ©John Sunderland

First Edition 2025

Published by Shilka Publishing
ISBN: 978-1-80443-094-1

TABLE OF CONTENTS

Preface i

Introduction—A New Life 1

Pepe's Giant *Patata* 10

Painting Tears and Joy.. 16

Closed All Hours 26

The Last Shepherd's Dog 30

Paw Camp 58

The Village Late May... 77

Three Men on a Step (and Other Meanderings) 78

Shopping for News 91

A Tad Less.. 94

Steel Mules 100

Dog Blankets 106

Market Mornings.. 111

Silla Season or the Wrong End of the Stick........................... 114

The Menace of Melons	119
Prickle Scratch Sting	124
Pixie Painters	130
Sleeping with Siesta	133
Picasso At My Door	137
Summer's Children	141
A Simple Life	145
On Tour with The Duchess	148
No Rain in Spain	162
Walk	166
Hammocked	169
Laundry in Foreign Parts	174
Pressing Times	175
A Lesson in the Garden	183
Up In Smoke	189
A Walk in the Words	192
Another Terrible Beautiful Day	208
Morning Bell	212
Of Dogs and Saints and Cemeteries	214
Rubbish	218
Reaper Called	220
There's No Smoke Without Firewood	222

Dust 227

A Case of The Vapours 230

Whiter Than White 232

A Crematorium and a Church 235

Dental Dave and the Mystery of the Telly Tooth 237

The Thing 242

End of an Era 243

Pascual's Tale 245

The Beautiful Time 264

Pascual and The Lord of the Kingdom of the Mountains 266

Epilogue 276

Acknowledgements 280

About The Last Shepherd's Dog 283

About the Author 284

Up the wiggly windy
Go the two old men
Up and down
And round the town
Then back home again

Preface

A word about the origin of this book.

Kath and I had developed the writing habit over the preceding years. Starting in 1980 I have kept up my journals, the daily scribble part of my morning ritual, hand-written with pen and ink, sometimes while half asleep. In some, written just after getting up before dawn, you can hear me yawning. I wrote about the totally new experiences we were having. So, recording daily short stories, accounts and observations came as second nature.

I write and draw in hardbacked journals (160 of them to date) making comments and sketches about my experiences, rather than just noting things as in a diary. Doing so makes me more aware of what's happening in my tiny sphere, and how things in the larger world affect my experience.

I decided to share. Several days a week I posted stories about moving to Tàrbena on my Facebook page from 2016. My intention was to entertain our friends and fellow villagers who, to my surprise, began following the fake virtual newspaper I'd dreamt up, which I called after the village we moved to, *Tàrbena Times*.

I wrote about what amused, interested, or bemused me from the previous day about our new life; spontaneous musings, not intended for a book.

I like writing, always have. The daily habit became a cathartic exercise, more self-therapy at first then communication. I had a technique; if something happened of interest, or was funny, it could be something simple, I'd note it down. The next morning, usually between five a.m. and eight, I'd write it up as a short account and post it on Facebook. They were random happenings and observations of life in a foreign land.

My wife went bonkers. She quickly realized I was putting raw mental meat out there without much, if any, concern for grammar, punctuation, etc. I liked the spontaneity, even though it was unprofessional. Readers didn't seem to mind.

Over time the stories mounted up into a collection of almost two hundred. *Tàrbena Times* took on a life of its own. Readers and responders were not only from the other side of the village or mountain but the other side of the planet.

I had no idea if there would be any interest. To my amazement I found that there was, and people would comment, even those I didn't know. I discovered the most seemingly ordinary things, when shared, could generate interest and delight.

So, I kept writing about ragbag topics of life in our rural village. The readership continued to grow, and a dialogue developed. That made me happy. I am glad the stories made the readers happy too.

Kath suggested we pick out the best ones, polish them up, add a comma and a full stop here and there and put them in a book. And so, this is it.

One subject I never tired of visiting is our adopted retired sheep and goat herding dog, Pascualet, "Little Pascual", the name every soul in the village calls him. By calling him Pascual we made him ours. He's been a feature of life here since he was a puppy, born to his job, as his mother was the shepherd's working dog too. Several stories of our life together and our adventures are at the core of this book.

He's fifteen years old now, an old dog. Our walks are slower, shorter, closer to home, lasting fifteen minutes or so, the most he can manage. This book is my legacy to the love, joy and companionship he has given us.

And something else: sharing countless hours in the campo with him, roaming the hills, forests and mountains in which he'd lived semi-wild. He showed me things I would never have seen or sensed.

I know it sounds crazy, but I believe, it was my dog who taught me Spanish.

John Sunderland
22 October 2023
Tàrbena, Alicante, Spain

Introduction—A New Life

My American wife Kathy and I boarded the Queen Mary II cruise liner in September of 2012 from a dock onss New York Harbour. It was near where we had been living together and she had her café bars, Life Café, which had in that year unexpectedly, thanks to the landlords, come to the end of their lives.

As Old Blue Eyes crooned, "New York, New York" over the ship's loudspeakers, we said "Goodbye, Goodbye," sipped our champagne and looked eastward to the open sea before us. We were relieved to be leaving New York City, an insatiable animal that can hold you in its thorny grip and suck you dry.

Here we were in our sixties, a Yank and a Tyke. We had arrived at an unplanned and unexpected early retirement. Where to go, what to do? We decided to try a new life in Europe and specifically Spain.

On that sunny, sharply lit, glamorous September afternoon upon the broad deck of a beautiful new ocean-going liner, little could we know what lay ahead. As we crossed the boundary shadow of the majestic Verrazzano Bridge on our way to the Atlantic Ocean, our lives were about to be changed by a totally different outlook.

I am a Yorkshireman (for those who may not know, Yorkshire is a county in the North of England). Kath, my wife, is a native of Detroit and lived the last thirty-two years in New York City. We're both retired. In my career I was a graphic designer, film maker, animator, and museum designer. Before my museum work, as an animator for Yorkshire TV, I created the cartoon character Dusty Bin and the show titles for the TV show 3*2*1. My initial museum job was as Project Designer of the original Jorvik Viking Centre in York, UK, which opened in 1984.

Two years earlier around 1982 in New York City, Kath and her first husband, David Life, gave birth to Life Cafe in New York City's East Village which was featured in the Broadway musical RENT by Pulitzer Prize winning Jonathan Larson. She opened a second place in Bushwick, Brooklyn, called Life Café 983. Kath had to close both restaurants in 2012, because of disputes with landlords.

A new life beckoned. We had lived together for several years in New York City and, facing the possibility that both businesses were about to close, we explored living in Mexico or Ecuador, common retirement destinations for Americans.

I mentioned this to my sister, Ann, and her husband Terry. They were retired from careers in the UK and suggested we come instead to southern Spain where they lived. Sunny welcoming Spain is a popular destination for Brits, as Florida is for Americans. My sister was right; don't disappear totally from sight, come home at least to Europe. It's where your family lives. In her opinion, Mexico would be too far away, and we were not getting any younger.

My sister arranged a cosy and comfortable rental house for the next eleven months, down the street from where they lived. The owners would come for a holiday in the twelfth month. By then, we realized life on a mainly British expat urbanization wasn't for us. It wasn't Spain, it was little Britain, built in a desert bowl next to a massive pig farm. But for many of the villa owners, it was a dream come true.

We started looking for a life experience in the real *España*. Kath saw an ad in the classified section of a free English language newspaper for an artist's house to rent further north, not far from the Mediterranean Sea, inland from the historic coastal town of Altea. The ad was enticingly illustrated with a tiny photo of a romantic *casa* (house), semi-tropical trees, cacti, mountains, and surrounding land.

"Waddya think?" Kath pointed to the photo in the ad that offered the Garden of Eden with a nice house for rent. We drove up, met the owner, a German lady and herself every centimetre the Artist, and thought the house quite magical. Soon after this, we moved in amongst the orange groves in a kind of dream, but with feet on the ground enough to finish my first book, *On My Way to Jorvik*, about the creation of the original Jorvik Viking Centre in York, England.

Tiny, medieval Bolulla, cradled by the surrounding craggy mountains, was the nearest village. To reach the house we had to drive on a single-track road praying as we went for a clear passage. Mostly, our prayers worked, but many times Kath's special abilities as a stunt driver in difficult and dangerous spots saved us from an inglorious screaming end.

It was challenging, it was wonderful, it was plantain trees outside the bedroom window, and alien insects in your clothes airing out at the end of the bed.

An artist's house was the perfect step into another realm. As we wrote and edited, celebrated our second Christmas in Spain, it felt as though we were living inside a beautiful, dream-like painting. Although it wasn't home, it was far enough away from the tarry rooftops of our apartment building in Brooklyn that, for us, was paradise.

We spent six months there finishing my book. We went to sleep dreaming, we woke up, and the dream continued. The rent was relatively high, but half what we paid in New York, so we were content for the time being.

The kitchen tap started to drip and got worse. The ultraviolet water purifier had to be replaced and the landlady said she wasn't going to do it because of the cost. That got us wondering, why there was such an elaborate water purifier there in the first place?

"What? Then what are we supposed to do for drinking water?"

"Go to the fonts in Bolulla and Tàrbena for water as everyone else does."

We looked at each other. Kath pulled me aside. "Water from the ground pure enough to drink? Free? Could that be possible?"

The next day we began exploring those very villages on the mountain, in search of the drinkable water flowing from *fuentes* (fountains) in the walls. In Tàrbena I counted seven of them. Each had a different name, history, and original purpose. Two had troughs for mules and farm animals to drink from. There is one the locals call *Font Del Botó*. It was the first we discovered down some shallow steps off the lane with a spectacular view of the mountains beyond.

We stood mesmerised first by the sound of running water. Liquid crystal spouted from an ancient carving on a trough fashioned from one piece of stone. The water gushed out of a pipe in the middle. I couldn't imagine how much had flowed from it over decades, maybe centuries, so much so that the pipe had partly worn away. The spouting liquid poured in a glassy arc and joined the water in the trough where it collected before draining into the hidden water system below. The sunshine infused the water with energy and life. It was beautiful. After years in the Big Apple, separated from nature, where little was free, it didn't seem possible, but here it was. What we hadn't yet grasped was that we were looking at the *liquid of life* of the village and it was ours to share. A pure, generous gift from mother nature.

Under a watery spell, we stood together and slowly turned around to take in the panorama, equally magical. Living our first few months immersed in meeting a publication deadline for a book, surrounded as we worked by orange groves, we hadn't yet explored our surroundings further up. Where we were in the landscape was unknown to us at that point. As we stood there, with the water flowing like a gift from heaven and the same light illuminating the most beautiful mountains with the bluest sea below, we wondered if we had died on the way up that precipitous road, gone over the edge, and this paradise is where we'd been granted our afterlife. It would do.

A few days later, back at our rental, the owner, realising we were fit to go, suggested we could clean the filter on the pipe which provided the house with water. Talking about this with people we'd met in the local pub, we discovered this was agricultural water. We were paying a considerable monthly amount for the privilege.

Time to go.

What followed over the next few days seemed like a series of connected miracles. Within days of falling in love with the waters of Tàrbena and the look of the village itself, we found a house to rent just along that very same lane as *Font Del Botó*.

We'd stumbled upon our little corner of heaven. If we were in fact deceased, it was turning out to be very nice.

Tàrbena was something of a mystery. We took a chance on all that we hadn't yet seen about the place, beyond the house and the *fuentes*. We knew nothing about the village and landscape beyond. We needn't have worried; we were in for more wonderful surprises.

It looked pleasant enough and interesting, perched on the rim of its mountain pass, looking down on the winding road below like a great uneven smile. You wouldn't call it picturesque. But, having said that, it was real, not a tourist trap, a place where people lived and worked, and the community functioned for a common aim.

Tourists did come and go, rarely staying long. The foundation wasn't tourism, it was agriculture, the main crops being almonds and olives. Of lesser economic importance were oranges, lemons, apples, cherries, carob, persimmon, avocado, and loquats, the last a big seasonal earner and a favourite with the Japanese.

The area was green and fertile and, unlike down on the coast, blessed with its own water supply. The surrounding limestone mountains soak up the rain and hold it inside like a rock sponge, slowly and naturally releasing it. We learned that the locals believe the village has enough H2O to survive the worst drought for three years. That is one the main reasons why a new village was founded here in the 1600's—water.

The climate, though unpredictable, also seemed to favour the area. They say there are on average 325 sunny days on the Costa Blanca a year. When we looked out of the windows of our new place, what we saw was a dramatic mountainous landscape painted with a big green brush.

The Costa Blanca Mountains reach heights over three thousand feet, and higher in some cases. The peaks and valleys mix up the air that flows over it and every now and then clouds roll in enveloping us in mist. There were tumultuous storms so intense, I had never seen the like before, storms which looked as though they could wash the whole mountain top away and down into the sea.

Storms or no storms, since we have lived here, there has never been enough water in the tanks. No matter how much one might dump, in the time we've been here, we have not met a farmer who has anything kind to say about the local climate, but then, isn't that the same with farmers everywhere?

It took us a while to realise the specialness of the village, some time for the penny to drop. There are pretty houses, quaint windy streets, back alleys, and lanes; a square, usually filled with parked cars and tractors. In addition, there are community buildings and a couple of shops.

What at first you don't quite get is that just up the street then along the track, and a bit further on the stony path beyond the olive grove, there is the most astonishing untouched wild landscape. When it is revealed to you for the first time, it takes your breath away. And it's just five minutes from your front door, free, yours, ours to share.

I've lived in some fantastic places on the North Yorkshire Moors where most years Siberia came to visit in winter. On Cape Cod, Massachusetts, overlooking the sea where Humpback whales would pay a call and blow you a steamy Christmas greeting as you stood at the sink doing the morning washing up. And, in New York City, say no more.

But nothing quite like this.

Just over the rim of the hill directly in front of our house is a wild and wonderful mountain range. It was originally the Mediterranean seabed, then plates shifted and lifted as the land masses collided. After eons of time sculpted by rain and wind, we see them as great big pointy mountains. It's this landscape, in the bosom of which this little village sits, which makes it so very special. And its glorious climate, air so fresh I swear it cleans your teeth and lungs every time you suck it in!

When we arrived there were many buildings left empty around the village, some of which were showing signs of sad neglect. Locals and long-term residents would tell you that the place was dying. Young people left for further education and opportunities which they could never have here in a small agriculturally based village. There was little work to be had; the farming, like the houses, was in decline, the world had moved on, almost medieval farming practices couldn't keep pace. Apart from a few days here and there and summer weeks of vacation, the houses handed down for generations stood quiet and empty, bones of a past now gone.

Melancholia tinges the air and darkens the shadows. We felt for the village as a whole as it seemed it was dying under our feet. The old residents and locals told us, "It's for the old folk now. When they have gone, it too will go."

On the surface, the place still looked interesting, and the landscape was just as stunning. But living here, what would happen if the decline continued, and one day it rolled over and died as the last funeral bell tolled and with us still alive in it? The thought haunted me. I used to think after we'd moved into the old house we bought, perhaps we were going against the grain. After all, people were moving out, not moving in.

We were wrong to think that; we were members of a vanguard, people who longed for fresh air, pure water, and a community just like this.

It took a while, but then, rather than a village in its death throes, Tàrbena began to look more like a village granted a new life. Many European expats were attracted here and chose a more natural life off grid. Others were delighted at the prospect of living part of the year at least, in the village, in a painted house on one of the wiggly windy streets, all hills and turns, back-alleys and lanes.

The derelict empty houses have slowly begun to be repaired, fixed up and improved. The streets have sprouted planters full of flowering plants. New faces appear in the local shops. People have arrived who want a share in its wonderful bounty. Tàrbena was beginning to experience a renaissance. We had arrived just at the right time.

Pepe's Giant *Patata*

When my wife and I first arrived in this unspoiled farming village hidden in the Costa Blanca Mountains, we rented a commodious 1920s house. It had nineteen rooms, including wine cellar, space for the mule and the tractor (we hadn't packed either of those), and a garage that would convert into a studio.

That garage was a huge part of my attraction to the place. It was accessible from the outside, and had large sliding windows, through which the most beautiful mountains were visible, a source of unending inspiration. In full view was the ruin of the Moorish Castillo de Tàrbena, the Tàrbena Castle, silhouetted on the crest of a craggy ridge, built hundreds of years ago to watch for invaders from afar. The panorama was priceless and the rent reasonable, so we moved in and lived there for our first year.

I like to paint and, shortly after moving in, I developed a passion for carving walking sticks from local woods. As with most men, I lusted after my own 'shed' out of range of my wife's organisational attentions. She called the garage my manhole. I quickly installed my easels, paints, carving gear and myself.

An artist needs north light. To get it all day, I had to keep the garage door open. That was a good thing because curious locals could see in. We wondered how friendly they would be and how long it would take us to be accepted.

Our village, Tàrbena, has been isolated for most of its history. Even today, you drive up the mountain road with trepidation. There are 75 bends (I counted them) on the way up and almost all come with a sheer drop on one side.

The local population of only 500 are pretty much a law unto themselves. There is a small energetic community of expats. Besides British there are Dutch, German, Swiss, Belgian, French, Czech, Norwegian, people from all parts of Europe, who in the main have been here for considerable periods of time. We were newbies to them as well as to the born and bred.

Would we, an ex-New Yorker (my wife Kath) and me, a Yorkshireman, also via New York City, be accepted? We very much wanted to be a part of a real Spanish community.

Outside the garage door, there's a steep and cracked concrete ramp. At the top of the ramp there's the village open-air laundry where spring water drains into a long, heavy trough where the washing used to be, and still occasionally is, done. Below it, strips of land descend like a green staircase into the steep valley below.

One day, a few weeks into our stay, I used the first word I'd learned in Spanish: *hola*. I called it out to a man who I thought was our neighbour from across the road. I'd seen him working his plot of land below my studio. "*Hola!*" I repeated. It had no effect on him, much to my disappointment and concern. He didn't even look my way, just walked on, buckets in hand. I thought, "Crikey, they don't like us already and they don't even know us!"

Over the next few weeks, as he and other locals carried on with their lives as though we didn't exist, Kath and I remained in our little personal village of two. We began to doubt we'd done the right thing in coming to such a place. In New York City, where we lived for eight years, surrounded and crammed in with millions more people, you are always an island, a bubble in the crowded streets. No one looks at you, no one speaks to you, everybody is a stranger. Here in Tàrbena, if you don't say hello to everyone on the street, they think there's something wrong with you. You can end the day with an aching jaw and tired eyes just from looking at people and smiling. If we wanted to be part of the village, we just had to bide our time and find ways to contribute to the community.

We had, however, made friends with a lovely local English lady, Diane. She had been here for twenty-nine years, before they paved the road and piped the water. I told her how we were having a hard time making contact with the locals.

"Give them time. They're watching you and they're curious."

I also told her how our neighbour seems to ignore me when he passes on his way by my studio.

"That's Pepe," she laughed. "He's as deaf as a post! Do something to attract his attention, and shout."

Then one day, Pepe of the buckets and the vegetable patch, slowly climbed the ramp. He was bent over with the weight of two large rubber buckets called *capazos* and was oblivious of me.

Emboldened by a late afternoon glass of *vino*, I thought, "Bugger it. If they won't come to us, then I'll go to them." I stepped out from the sanctity of my manhole to greet him in person. I was also nosey as to what he had in the buckets that was worth all his effort.

"*Hola!*" I yelled, louder than before at the top of the ramp. This time he turned his head and smiled a little and nodded. I stepped toward him, wiping my painted hands on my apron, and held one out. He stopped and put down a bucket.

Finally, a response. "*Hola.*"

He had a tanned, stubbled farmer's face. Though a man of senior years, he had the strongest handshake, and I feared I'd never hold a paintbrush again.

I thought, I've got to keep this going. He nodded again, and as he bent to pick up the buckets, I looked into one. It was filled with huge potatoes. Just one of them could have made chips for an average junior school for a week. I pointed at them. "By gum. Fantastic!"

At this, he smiled and looked at me, shaking his head a little sadly, as though thinking I'd never seen a potato before. Then he picked up the buckets and carried on. I went back to my canvas. Contact! Even if it was because of a bucket of spuds.

The next day I was trying to imagine myself as Picasso, but basically wasting canvas, paint, and time as I'm not, when I felt a presence behind me. I turned round and there was Pepe, framed by the doorway.

He was holding the most enormous potato I'd ever seen, probably that had ever been grown on the planet, almost as large as a rugby ball. He held it out to me as he said something, I had no idea what. Sensing that, he thrust it out to me again. It was a gift! One in which he obviously took great pride. He'd grown this amazing thing from his dirt, working with his horny old hands. It was his pride and joy, and as I accepted it, I realised it was worth more than its weight in gold. It couldn't have been a better gift.

"*Gracias*," the second useful word I'd learned. He said something else, turned and walked away.

I stood there with Pepe's giant potato. Back home in New York City, it would have had its own cooking show. Then, staring up at the bluest driest sky, I wondered; how could he grow such a thing? Big as a toddler's head, what on earth could we do with it? It was too wonderful to make chips or mash from. Then I had an a-ha moment.

Off came the crap paint daubing on the easel, to be replaced by a pristine canvas. Onto a high stool next to me went the potato. I might not be a genius painter, but I sure know how to paint.

Kath had seen Pepe from the kitchen window upstairs. She came down. "So, how's your *amigo*?" She spotted the enormous entity on the stool, "Lordy be, that's a big one!"

"It's Pepe's giant ..." and before I could say the word, she exclaimed, "*patata*."

"Yes, Pepe's giant *patata*. And I'm going to paint its portrait."

She looked at me. "I think I'll take the wine upstairs now."

Two days later, Pepe was coming up from his plot. Standing at the garage door, I greeted him, "Hola." By my side was a medium size canvas on the easel with its back to us.

"Pepe!" I shouted. He came over and leant on his mattock. I turned the canvas round. "For you."

His jaw dropped. There was a pause and a clang as the mattock fell to the ground. I passed the painting to him.

"It's a portrait of Pepe's Giant *Patata*!"

We weren't remotely sharing the same language but, as they say, a picture speaks a thousand words. He held it as though he'd just been handed the holy grail as a birthday present.

It hangs framed on the wall of his sitting room, almost three years on now, beside a portrait of a giant eggplant, an enormous shapely lemon that reminded me of Marilyn Monroe, and soon they will be joined by a gigantic onion.

That day, as he took the painting home to show his wife, a door opened for us. We'd taken our first steps into this wonderful community on the mountain, and all due to a potato—sorry, *patata*!

June 2014

Painting Tears and Joy

Today, I returned a portrait I painted for a family here in the village. They commissioned it a couple of years ago. After it was completed and handed over to them, they returned it to me not long after, badly damaged.

Fortunately, I was able to refer them to a specialist in a nearby town, L'Alfàs del Pi, who could repair the canvas. Once done, I suggested they bring it back; I would fix the paint surface and do my best to make it look as it had originally. The painting had come to mean a lot to the family, and indeed to me. It has a story.

Two summers ago, a woman came into my studio. She was the sister of a lady who lived and worked in the village. Though she didn't speak English and my Spanish is less than poor, we communicated with the help of a friend. She had seen some of my work and asked me if I painted portraits. I said I did, at which point she opened her purse and produced a passport photo in a little translucent envelope.

Through my interpreter friend, she told me the photo was of her husband taken years ago, I think around the time they'd met. He was much younger, probably in his early thirties. He was a strikingly handsome man, who in his fifties, had succumbed to cancer. She and her family were heartbroken.

There were tears in her eyes as she asked me in Spanish, "Can you make a painting from this? It is all I have."

I felt the hope in the question and the emotion that went with it. This would be no ordinary commission and it would be a huge responsibility.

I took the photo in my fingers. It was extremely tiny. How could I work from such a small image? But there was something intense about it. The way he looked out of it, so very alive. You know how we look flat in those passport photos? This was different.

With some trepidation, I agreed, explaining that it would take the best part of a month. She understood and went away happy. It was going to be a hell of a challenge, and I felt I was taking on more than just a painting.

The lady, his widow, had a lovely way about her, a radiant warmth. She wanted nothing less than for me to bring her husband of twenty-five years back to life, and she seemed to beam that hope right at me.

And the village would be watching.

Portraits are difficult. Although ostensibly you're out to capture a likeness, which may be painfully honest or flattering, you're also out to capture a sense of the person. Even though you may not actually know or have met him or her, you attempt to reach beyond the skin, hair, and cloth to touch and reveal the individual.

It can go horribly wrong. A few years back in New York City, where my wife had two restaurants, Stephen, an East Village regular who lived upstairs, asked if I would like to paint his portrait. I was flattered and took it on. He was a writer of political opinion as well as a book illustrator with a conservative, classical bent. But in himself, permanently depressed; a dark damp cloud seemed to hang over him and the bar.

Getting on with it, I took several photos and a preparatory drawing from life and then started. Only a few hours into it, I'm afraid my feelings took over and dripped through the brush, spilling out onto the canvas. I felt, though, it was also going to be an excellent portrait, but uncompromising.

Once completed, we had a little unveiling at the restaurant.

Off came the cover. Whatever the others thought of the piece, the one person whose appreciation I sought was the subject himself. Deep down, I think I was hoping to cheer him up.

Unfortunately, when he recognized his true self in the portrait, it had the opposite effect. It was too honest. His vanity was dashed to the floor; he was mortified, completely speechless. The painting showed him as the world saw him. Well, at least through my possibly tainted vision. The artist's eye and mind can be a distorting filter. A true professional portraitist would have been able to control his feelings but, with Stephen, I had succumbed to my own. It's a good painting and we kept it and brought it to Spain. He still looks miserable on our wall even though the sun shines and oranges fall free and happy from the trees.

In a way, he had his revenge as we live with his sad face every day.

Back in the village of Tàrbena up on the mountain, the painting of the man in the passport photo had taken weeks to complete, during which something quite extraordinary happened.

As I said, I'd no experience of the man in the photo apart from this small image, which I carefully attached to the easel. What else did I know about him? I knew his widow had loved him very much and clearly still did. She and the rest of their family missed him. I came to think of him as a good man, well liked and respected and with a powerful presence and personality, which, the more I looked at it, shone out through the little photo.

His nephew, a lovely lad in his pre-teens, came in a couple of times for sneak previews as I worked, but I kept the canvas out of view.

You're going to think I'm right out of my tree now, but as I worked on this handsome mesmerizing face, he seemed to come to life, a sort of raw resurrection happening on the canvas. It got to a point when I found it very difficult to maintain objectivity, often painting through the blur of my own tears. The experience was becoming emotionally draining. I felt as though I could sense this man's pain. Imagination and projection maybe, but it felt real.

I wondered if I was having some kind of psychic experience and every day I went to paint, he was getting stronger. More than just a likeness, there was a soul there, appearing through the ether, looking out from the painting as though from the opposite side of a two-way mirror.

His face charged the canvas with an energy, crazy as it sounds, an emotion powered by a huge sad anger at being taken from his family too early in life.

It was getting to me and I wasn't sure whether I had what it would take to finish, but I couldn't leave him in limbo, could I? He needed to reach out and this portrait was his conduit.

Having taken on a commission to paint the portrait of a deceased man from a passport photo, the painting was giving the artist not technical problems but emotional paranoia.

When you create a painting, especially a portrait, you reach a point where you know whether it's working. It's when the thing takes on its own life, the birthing. That's certainly a joyous place to get to.

It happened for me when I'd completed his eyes. It was as though he could see; the portrait was looking out into my studio at the observer, not the opposite way round. To be honest, it was kind of spooky, as every day I worked with those eyes looking out at me.

Visitors came to my studio, curious about what I was working on. I was able to keep the portrait under wraps as far as his family was concerned, but I couldn't stop others from sneaking a peek. It was difficult to keep this project private when the canvas had to be angled towards the north light that came through the large door open to the village.

Of all the paintings visitors had seen me working on, this one stopped them in their tracks. They were transfixed. The gaze from the canvas riveted children, seniors, locals of all ages. Somehow, it was more than a painting.

Then I finished it, and gosh was I pleased as well as emotionally exhausted. I invited the Spanish lady who had commissioned it to come to see it and hopefully approve it.

The moment a painting is revealed to the person who commissioned it is very significant and not without risk. You, the artist, want them to like it, to take it home, live with it, come to love it over time. It will live in their home for ever, you hope. Often it doesn't happen that way and, if you've spent weeks creating something and it's rejected, you feel rejected too.

There were high emotional stakes at play here. Would his wife see in the portrait what she was hoping for, more than just a memorial, a spark of his life through his countenance in paint?

I amplified the moment of reveal by making an event out of it.

The appointed time came and three people arrived; the lady, her woman friend from the village who helped translate, and the nephew, who had been coming to see how it was going on.

I set it on an easel and covered it with a cloth, then placed a wicker settee in front. They arrived, a little nervous, as was I. Sitting them comfortably all together in front of the easel, I pulled down the garage door part way, turning the garage into a private salon.

In anticipation that they may not be happy with it, I'd arranged through my interpreter friend not to charge my fee. Instead, I would keep the painting. But payment was the last thing on anyone's mind.

"Will you all please close your eyes," I said. The friend knew enough English to explain. "And not open them until I ask you to."

They closed their eyes. I waited a few seconds, removed the cover, then asked them to open.

They looked at the painting as if one body. There was utter silence, a moment of high tension. I was standing behind and to the side, holding onto the back of the wicker chair. Time stood still. The portrait in front seemed to look at his wife and family. It was a transcendent moment.

Then an amazing thing happened. The boy leant over to the lady's shoulder in a very child-like way, and began to sob, low at first, then uncontrollably. Then one lady started to cry, then another, all three sobbing on the wicker seat. Then I started. Four people in a garage sobbing in unison! And it didn't stop. In the end, we were all in a tearful hug.

Of course, being the paranoid neurotic I am, the thought crossed my mind that they were crying because they thought the portrait was awful. But no, quite the opposite; it had touched them in a way so deep it had entered their souls.

I learned some time later that the nephew of the man in the portrait loved him very much and had shown no emotion since he'd died. Rather, he'd bottled up his feelings. That morning, his love for his uncle came flooding out.

Eventually, after a few minutes, someone smiled, then laughed, then we all did. We returned to reality. They were thrilled, and of course, so was I.

It was done. They would collect the painting later.

We shared kisses and hugs all round. Time to leave. I turned to pull up the garage door, which I hadn't closed completely, leaving a few inches open at the bottom. We all shook ourselves straight and wiped tearful red eyes. As I yanked the door up, it opened with a bang, as it does.

Outside the studio the empty open space was filled with the children of the village, friends of the boy. No doubt they'd heard the sobbing. They were all silent, everyone looking and wondering, full of expectation, gathered together of their own volition—the children, the life and the future of the village. The nephew smiled, then laughed, then the kids burst into chatter and laughter, as the man in the passport photo came home.

Several months passed, when one day the nephew of the deceased man (the lad who had been so upset at the presentation in my studio) came looking for me. He speaks a little English and I understand a little Spanish; he had a question. Could I repair damage to the painting? What damage? I asked if I could look at it to see if I could help.

When he and his father turned up and showed me the canvas, I couldn't believe my eyes! It had three large rips, not small holes, great big tears. To this day I don't know what happened, but whatever it was, it was drastic.

There was no way I could repair those tears. It required specialised skills, but I offered to do the paint repairs. It disappointed them I couldn't fix the canvas, but it's best to be honest. I referred them to a specialist in L'Alfàs del Pi.

After several months went by, the father, Antonio, knocked on our door. He'd brought the repaired painting. It was a fine job, apart from one area where a scar in white glue arched from the top of the head into the background. That was too ugly and had to go.

It took a couple of days to restore the surface, and though I couldn't remove the indentation in the canvas where the tear had been repaired, I could restore the paint and hide it. Indeed, if you didn't know it was there, you wouldn't notice it. The painting, after such drastic damage, was fully restored.

This, however, is a story without an ending. I made phone calls and left messages saying I had restored the portrait. At the time of writing no one has collected it. It sits in our hall wrapped in brown paper waiting to be returned to its rightful owner.

The story of the painting of the man in the passport photo may not yet be over.

Postscript: Months after I had completed the restoration, the painting was finally retrieved. While I'd conjured up concerns as to what had caused such damage to the painting that everyone seemed to love, the answer was far more down to earth, literally. A family member explained that one of the ferocious gusts of wind that race through our narrow village streets had blown through an

open window in the house and knocked the painting off the wall. I know that is possible; paintings in my studio sometimes fly about like painted bats in those same blustery gusts.

May 2017

Closed All Hours

We had relatives visiting from Florida, USA, Laura and Joe, lovely people. Coming from a very different place and culture, they were a little surprised to discover that our village has only one small grocery shop serving the population of around five hundred. And they were even more surprised that the nearest supermarkets were down the mountain.

As there's no hardware store here, for example, if you need a new screwdriver or new bolt for the door, you have to go down then back up the precipitous and dangerous road, negotiating those bends on your return journey and assorted packs of brightly attired cyclists in training, slow-moving tractors and the occasional school bus depending on the time of day.

Not long ago, there were four shops and a tobacconist, who sold her nicotine wares from her front room. When we arrived, there were only two shops left. Only the strange thing was, one of them, which outwardly appeared to be a grocery shop, was always closed, even though temptingly stocked to the ceiling.

I am not privy to the story, and don't know the facts, but I ache with curiosity and nosiness every time I walk by because it's quite easy to see inside through the large windows. The lights are often on, as is a large flat-screen TV which hangs on a wall facing the street above a dining table positioned amongst the rows and stacks of toilet rolls.

More often than not, there's an American cowboy film showing with members of family and friends watching. Now, that's not particularly odd or eccentric; what is curious is that this is not a front room. It is, or was, a general store packed with stuff to sell like a grocery Mary Celeste.

There are shelves of bottles, jars and boxes, cling film and tuna, firelighters, cans of beans, mop heads, rubbish bags, light bulbs and bottles, cans of fizzy drinks, sauces. A fully stocked shop, apart, I expect, from frozen produce and customers. Otherwise, it has morphed for some mysterious reason into a front room. What happened? Did the owner suddenly wake up and decide not to bother anymore? And why keep the entire inventory on display? I'm not in any way being critical; it's just that as a former museum designer and storyteller, I'm fascinated with the surreality of the scene.

If the shop has been frozen in time for only a few years, it's already a museum piece. Products change, packaging is updated, new products can be expected. But here, as far as you can see as you walk by, the only fresh produce on offer is the past, and it's closed anyway, set in time after the last customer departed and the cash register banged shut.

Now John Wayne looks down on the unused counter, the unopened register, the stocked shelves, as nosy and curious incomers peek in ducking the bad guy's bullets flying amongst the tins of tomatoes.

I never found out why the shelves remained stocked for so long after the kindly elderly residents had retired. One can only assume they were comfy cosy as they were. Besides, it must have been handy to reach for a bag of peanuts.

But hang on, we can't just leave it there. How is one to sleep at night not knowing why the residents live in a shop? I thought about asking other locals about it, but that would be too intrusive and nosey. Besides which, my Spanish is not up to it. What about asking the people who live there directly? But how would you explain your curiosity and interest? When we were new to the village, Kath went in once for a bag of sugar. The lady who sits in the window shooed her out.

I came up with theories, fantasies, or fictional mysteries, which just might be true. Here's a few:

1. It's not real, it's an advanced holographic animation, an experiment in a remote village.
2. The residents just can't bear to part with their stock.
3. They needed to retire the shop but would miss it too much. So rather than collect photos of the past, they are living in it.

And my favourite....

4. They are hanging on to the stock until all the sell-by dates have expired. (Now that sounds reasonable.)

If those don't help, make up some of your own. Whatever the case, one day all the stock did disappear off the shelves, along with the shelves. Chairs and tables arrived and the shop became a more conventional living room. The big-screen TV remained.

May 2017

The Last Shepherd's Dog

1

It was November 2015, and the little old house we'd bought in the village had just become habitable after some much-needed reconstruction. We hired a British bloke, a talented carpenter/builder with electrical skills. He was an artist at it. His Spanish was good and he hired a crew of local craftsmen who knew their stuff. The renovation went smoothly over a few months. We finally had a home of our own

New York City, where we lived before coming to Spain, was behind us. We were retired and content, yet something was missing; the patter of tiny feet—four of them.

"Shall we get a dog?" I said over lunch. "Álvaro's terrier is having puppies."

Through a mouthful of salad, Kath objected. "They're all yaps and no fun."

"Make excellent guard dogs,"

"Make a pain in the neck. Why a terrier?"

"Well, Álvaro asked me if we were interested in one."

"See," she said nodding, "he wants to get rid of them."

"We always had a dog when I was growing up. And you had your greyhounds. You loved them."

"John. you have to take them for walks. And most likely that will become another of my jobs."

I wasn't to be discouraged. "No, it won't. Look, I'm overweight. With a dog you get exercise, take it for walkies every day. I'd love it!"

"Your wine barrel won't."

"You'll see. I'll get trimmer and slimmer."

"You'll need a team of huskies to get rid of that."

I'd be able to bring her round, I thought; just had to let sleeping dogs lie for a little while.

"Luna, that dog of Álvaro's, is cute," Kath said a couple of days later.

"Hmm, yappy though."

"Ok then. Tell him we'll take a puppy, but *you* feed it, take it to the vet, get up in the middle of the night when it has to go out, all that. It'll be your dog."

"Yes, promise. You know this is manifestation. We both wanted a dog."

She shook her head. "Not me."

"Secretly you did, and I did too. It'll make our life here complete, and one's turned up on our doorstep."

"A girl dog will be better. I'd prefer a bitch, loyal and loving. Asi was a bitch. She was special." Kath mellowed off into fond memories. "We'll have to get her stuff."

"It's not been born yet." The Yorkshireman in me was sensing a serious exit of euros.

"A dog basket, a bowl, no, two bowls, and a lead. And she'll have to have her shots and be wormed and spayed.

"Wait… er."

"We'll have it done, anyway, alright?"

Several weeks had passed when we heard via the village telegraph that Álvaro's dog had given birth to four puppies. Kath was arranging the new dog blanket in the wicker basket under the table. "They'll have to stay with their mother until they're weaned."

We waited. A couple of days turned into a week, and I was getting anxious. "They're only little dogs. I wonder how long it takes for them to finish weaning. I can't imagine it needing much milk to fill them up." Álvaro seemed to have disappeared from the village and Planet Canine.

"He hasn't forgotten us. He wouldn't do that, would he?" said Kath, "I saw little Maria in the square with the loveliest puppy in her arms, a terrier, and it looked as if its eyes had just opened. I wonder if it was one of Álvaro's."

"Oh, don't worry. I checked on the internet and it takes weeks before puppies can leave their mother."

Then I heard sad news. Salvador, the last shepherd of the village who had retired recently, had died unexpectedly. I told Kath.

"He seemed a nice man."

"I heard his dog was silent as the police broke down the door," I shared.

"They were lucky he didn't attack them! He seems fierce."

"I think he's too smart a dog for that."

Kath shook her head.

"Poor thing. Who's going to have the guts to take *him* on?"

I walked to my studio that evening. We hadn't known Salvador apart from getting to the "*Hola, bon día*" level of communication as we passed him in the square. But we could see his dog worshipped him. Dogs sense stuff about people.

"Laura says the funeral is tomorrow at eleven," I reported when home. "Sounds as if the entire village will be there."

"Any puppy news?" asked Kath from her desk.

"No, not a yap."

"Maybe Álvaro forgot about us."

"Well, fingers crossed."

In the meantime, expat animal lovers tried to convince us to take on Pascualet, Salvador's dog. At the Thursday market in the square Kath heard that Pascualet was a village dog, born and raised here, well known and loved, and it would be a shame if he was taken away. People hinted it would mean so much to the village if we could adopt him. We just smiled and said we might consider it, but Kath had her heart set on a puppy.

Spanish funerals happen within 48 hours, something to do with the hot dry climate. It was almost Christmas and as we opened the blinds, the new day was grim, grey, and drizzling. I went to get my rain parka.

"Great day for a funeral."

"Perfect," replied Kath.

The church bell tolled, which meant the religious service was over and the funeral procession would leave the square following the hearse. We joined at the top of the hill. Below, the white walls of the cemetery were visible through the mist.

As the mourners descended, umbrellas made an armadillo of the procession.

Beneath hers, Kath's voice was hushed. "I expect to see his dog down there, you know, with him to the end. They seemed devoted."

"Pascualet?"

"What?"

"Pascualet, that's what the villagers call him. Someone must have taken him in," I speculated.

"That would be like having a hungry crocodile in your kitchen! Rather them than us."

The cemetery is a beautiful and sacred place revered by all enclosed on all four sides with high white walls. You reach it by a narrow road, which descends from the main body of the village. On the outer edge of the community, its location, at the end of a lane and before a great pinnacle of rock with a sheer drop beyond, reminds the villagers of their final resting place.

Instead of graves in the ground, the deceased are placed in niches in the walls fronted with engraved monuments dressed with flowers and photographs of the deceased. Whole families are there, reaching back generations surrounded by tall sentinel yew trees. It's a very moving and peaceful place, sheltered but open to the bright sky.

The coffin bearers had brought Salvador's coffin to his spot, raised it, and tried to slide it into the niche; but it wasn't empty. Inside was a large stiff blue plastic bag.

"That's his brother," announced a voice in an Irish accent. It was Maggie, a friend and long-time resident of the village, as Irish as they come. "Yes, nice man. His brother Vicente died 15 years ago."

It happened that the *albañil* (builder) who bricks up the opening after the coffin is inserted was Álvaro. He shifted the bag to one side to make room, but the coffin still wouldn't fit. I wondered if Salvador had had a good relationship with his brother. Álvaro pulled the bag out, set it on the ground, put the coffin in, then stuffed the bag back in the remaining space.

Maggie leaned towards us. "I do hope they get on. They were always falling out, fights all over the square!"

The *albañil* began bricking up the opening in full view of the mourners, as is the custom. Umbrellas dripped; people hitched their collars up further as the drizzle made tears on stoic faces.

"I think I'd rather be under a duvet of earth and eaten by worms with a little salad," muttered Kath as we looked on for the very last time at the remains of a man we barely knew but somehow sensed a connection to.

A half-whispered voice close to my shoulder. "*Señor* John."

It was Javier, a pleasant young man and a partner of the bar in the square. He always had a ready smile, but there was none today. He looked up at the niche, being bricked up. "Sad. He was not long retired." He spoke in his best English as he shook my hand.

"Yes. It's moving. First time we've been to a village funeral." I placed my other hand on my heart. "We didn't know him, but somehow we liked him."

Javier was not alone, several more men had grouped around. He came closer, keeping hold of my hand. I was feeling awkward. He leant forward. "I have to tell you something," he whispered. "It is about an *offer*."

Suddenly I was talking with Don Corleone, and music from The Godfather echoed in my head as mist breached the graveyard walls and thickened around us.

"An *offer*?" Thinking food, I whispered back. "What? You mean a special price deal lunch at Bar Javier after this?" That was the name of their popular bar in the village square.

"No!" he recoiled and let go of my hand. "*Señor* John, please. This is a serious matter."

Kath sensed something was happening and turned her attention to us.

"So, what is it?" I asked. "*What* offer?"

"I am sorry to tell you, *Señor* John, there is no little puppy dog for you."

"You mean Álvaro's puppies?"

"No puppy?" said Kath in full voice. Mourners as one turned towards us.

"*Sí*, she has another home."

Kath shook her head. "Oh dear. That's sad. We were looking forward to her coming to us. We'd bought a basket and everything. Even a collar with her name on."

Javier's smile switched back on and with it his bright blues twinkled. "But there is *another* dog."

"Another puppy?" asked Kath.

"Er, no, not a puppy, more mature, a magnificent *animal*! He needs a home real bad. Salvador," he nodded his head toward the niche, "the man in the box was his owner. As you see, he is dead. *Los amigos* of Salvador have asked me to ask you, because of my English."

Kath was suspicious. "Oh, have they? Ask what?"

"If you could be a home for him?" pleaded Javier with hands outstretched.

I interjected. "But Javier, if his friends are concerned for the dog, why doesn't one of them give him a home?"

"Oh, John. Everyone knows the British are good with dogs. You love dogs for the home. Look at the Corgis!"

"He's a Corgi?" Kath brightened.

"No, Katy. I mean the dogs of your Queen." (In the Spanish language, it's difficult for people to pronounce "Kathy" with the "th" sound.) He straightened again. "All over the palace. You see,

Salvador has retired from the goats and so has Pascualet. He needs a home." He shifted on his feet. "The Spanish love their *animales* but in a place like this, they are farmers, and to them Pascualet is a working dog, and shall be always. Not a dog for the lap."

"Who?" I asked.

"*Pascualet*, the dog of which we speak, his name; it means Easter." He got serious again. "John, Katy, if you could a home for him give, Salvador," he nodded in the direction of the niche, "will sleep easier." He smiled sweetly for a moment, nodded, and closed his eyes, his hands raised in supplication. More people gathered around and looked at us with earnest expectation.

"But, but…is he domesticated?" I asked.

"¿Qué?" Javier's face was suddenly perplexed.

Kath jumped in. "Is he trained? You know, like to walk on a lead? Sleep in a basket? Fetch balls?"

Javier straightened up and flicked his chin. "Salvador trained him only to chase goats and bring them home."

"We don't have goats," I pointed out.

"And we're not getting any; they'd eat my petunias and carrots," added Kath.

"Alas, if no home," Javier put his hand on my shoulder, "it will be *muerte* for him at the dog's home. He will go crazy! To sleep they will put him." He drew his other hand across his throat.

"But he's a very active dog," objected Kath. "He's always running around and fighting. And we have such a tiny house."

Javier, unperturbed, smiled on. "Oh, but such an animal and *muy inteligente!*"

"He's a *real* dog, dog," I said to Kath, nodding. "He is." I was aware of his reputation. I'd also seen him running past my studio door, both ways, and he'd made an impression on me too. Although I wasn't about to admit it, I would stop painting to look as he passed; he always appeared to be on a mission, but what?

Javier turned to Kath under her umbrella. "Katy, we have seen you in the village, trying to make friends with him when he was running. Is that not so?"

"Yes. I thought he looked magnificent, but he ignored me."

"You never told me that," I complained.

She sighed. "We wanted a puppy, a little dog, that's all, one we could train."

I added, "We hadn't bargained on a lion! A little lion though, small as lions go."

Javier put his hand on my shoulder again, while rain dribbled down his face.

"This is a dog that is loved in the village. This place and the mountains are his home. If he doesn't find a home here, he will be dead soon. And I believe, *we believe,*" he gestured to the others around him, "Salvador's spirit will not rest." He shook his head, so did others. One lady pulled out a hanky nodded and dabbed her eyes.

He came closer under the umbrella. We were a crowd now under it.

I whispered to him, "Do your friends here understand English?" He ignored me, came even closer for what he was about to whisper in our two ears at once. "I speak to you as good and new friends. Listen to me, please. It is difficult for *extranjeros* (foreigners) to be accepted in such an old place as this. If you do this, the local people will love and respect you overnight."

He then turned to face the almost plastered niche. He must have sensed Kath and I needed to talk together. In the background, Salvador's coffin was almost gone from view. "Kath, listen," I murmured under the umbrella.

"What?" She was moved. "You know we're being walled up too, don't you?"

I drew her closer, "I didn't realise you have been watching this dog as well as me. He's not what we expected, *but* darling, what's that word…*serendipity? Fate, manifestation.* He could be perfect for us."

Unconvinced, Kath shivered. "He'll probably eat us! Look, Álvaro is smoothing the plaster over." Then she scanned around amongst the black patent shoes and the puddles. "I wonder where his dog is. You don't suppose he's in there with him, do you, like the Egyptians?"

I looked at her dead serious, and she at me.

"Come on, let's give him a try! Shall we? How about a walk tomorrow in the village to see what he's like? Then we'll give him back for the weekend and make up our minds after we've thought about it and tell them on Monday."

"It would be good to try him out," she ruminated. "All right. What's the worst that could happen? Say nothing!"

We both looked back at Javier.

"Would it be possible for us to take him for a short walk in the village tomorrow for a few minutes?"

"*No hay problema.* Anyway, there is the offer. Tonight, Pascualet stays with a friend of Salvador's. Have you met Jorge? He has him in his village house. Collect from there, say at ten o'clock tomorrow, is ok? Soon someone must decide. It is an offer of life or death!"

2

Jorge, who currently had the dog, was born here and no doubt would die here. He was not the friendliest towards us or to anyone else in the expat community, as I'd noticed. I couldn't blame him or the other villagers if they felt resentful toward outsiders who were settling in their once remote untouched community and couldn't speak their language properly.

When the next morning came, despite looking forward to seeing the dog and taking him for a test walk, I felt apprehensive about our human encounter.

As it was, it was no problem, as Jorge spoke no English and our Spanish was negligible. He opened the garage door to his house on the side of a steep lane. I got the impression that he, his wife, and the dog were glad to have a break from one another. The dog was barking his head off.

When he emerged, Pascualet was shaking and agitated. Jorge handed him over on a length of old rope tied round his neck, like a noose. I stroked his sides to calm him down, but to no avail. The garage door closed. We put a collar and lead on him given to us by one local who heard we might take him on. Pascualet didn't complain when I put it on; he was too mixed up and confused. He didn't even growl.

"Come on, boy."

I dropped to my haunches and looked him in the eyes. Then he growled, so I backed off and stood up.

"We are going for a little walk," Kath told him. He waved his tail.

Kath watched him closely. "He doesn't understand what we're saying."

"Of course, not we're not speaking *Valenciano*."

Kath touched my arm. "Make your voice calm and reassuring. I think he's suffering from separation anxiety; he's just lost Salvador. Having been locked up in the house with the body for two days. And who knows what went on in there? She nodded to the house. "Look how he's trembling. Let's show him some kind discipline."

We collected him between us. Walking down the hill together felt right. In fact, I felt warm inside. But Kath wore a frown as she watched the dog; she was concerned. He was twirling and jumping at the end of the lead, as though electricity was running through him, stepping on our feet and tripping us.

I held his lead tightly. "This is not a wild animal. This is a frightened confused dog."

Kath had some experience training the greyhounds she had years ago in America. Two were show dogs and lead trained. "Here, let me take the lead. He's going to be a lot of work. He's traumatised and untrained. I'm not sure if we're up to the effort. We're starting our life over too." She had a point.

The walk was nearing its end when Kath's arm jerked back. She came to a standstill, as Pascualet squatted and left a large gooey brown pile right in front of the *panadería*, the bread shop. Embarrassed, Kathy disappeared inside to apologise and came out with a plastic bag to clean up the mess.

We had walked ten minutes one way and about the same time back a different way and rang the doorbell of Jorge's house. Pascualet whimpered at the sound. When the garage door reopened and Jorge appeared, the whimper had become a howling bark. I offered the rope lead to Jorge as Pascualet strained in the opposite direction.

I bent down and spoke our last words to him for that day.

"Pascualet." He looked me in the eye and this time no growl. "We'll be back soon. We'll come for you; I promise boy."

Kath squeezed my shoulder. "I think he understood that." We walked a bit.

"We need to talk about this John."

As the garage door lowered like the drawbridge to a castle prison, Pascualet roared and cried in anguish.

"God!" said Kath, as we hurried away. "I feel as though my heart is being ripped out!"

"I feel the same." Each step down the hill became slower and our legs heavier.

"Do you fancy a drink?" I asked as we approached the square.

"Yes, a stiff one, but I can't stop tearing up."

"Me, neither. Two stiff ones."

We ordered two brandies at Bar Javier.

"It's true, what Javier said. From the Queen down, we Brits are dog lovers; it's in our genes."

Spanish bars are noisy. It was welcomed. We hid in a corner inside the noise.

"We can't let him go to the shelter; he'll be put down for sure," I said. "He's wonderful but scared to death. That's intelligence, he's no mutt." The brandies arrived, Kath reached across the table and took my hand. "We'll have him then. But just to say; now that we have walked with him, I see him differently. He's going to be more than a handful for me. He's strong and muscular, agile, untrained, semi-wild and going to need dedication. We weren't planning on this. He'll be a life changer, far more than just a pet." She paused. "He needs serious work, and maybe he's past learning."

Our eyes met.

"But I'm willing to give him a chance. I *want* to give it a go, but we have to do this together, totally, alright? If you dump him on my lap, I'll take him down the mountain myself."

We gestured to Javier to pay. He came over to take our money and find out how things had gone. His face, as usual, was one big smile with sparkling blue eyes like a TV game-show host, only it was expectant.

I put my arm around Kath's shoulder and looked up at Javier. "We are going to have him." We nodded in unison.

His face lit up. "Oh. This is *great* news." The bar went quiet. "You won't regret it, it may take a little time, but you won't, I promise!" He disappeared for a moment. "Here, on the house, *a mis amigos*."

He brought two more brandies and instantly, the entire bar was aware. Some men looked us up and down and shook their heads.

An elderly gnarled farmer, brown as the bar, standing next to us, turned and spoke over his glass in the impenetrable local dialect, a variety of *Valenciano* with a few words of *Mallorquí* added in. Javier translated, much to our relief.

"He says, never let him off the rope because if you do, he will be gone forever."

The old man waved his hand in the air as if a bird was taking flight over the mountains.

A voice in my head said, "One day, some place, there will be no reason for a rope."

Sunday morning arrived. Looking a little bleary as I peeked through the crack in the bathroom door I asked, "Honey, do you want to come for a walk? I'm checking out a dog route and thought you might want to come?" She made a sound in reply as if she was drowning in a quicksand of toothpaste.

Hills and mountains surround Tàrbena and closer in, tracks, lanes and paths emerge snake-like from the dry-stone walls. You can roam for hours and never be more than a couple of kilometres away from the main square, and yet believe you're the only person left in the world. But this morning I wasn't.

I bumped into Juan, considerably younger than me, who works as an engineering consultant down on the coast. I always thought he was a local because he seemed to speak the language well, but I learned he came to Tàrbena in his early teens with his parents.

He had his adored rescue dog, ginger biscuit-coloured Canela, with him. They emerged from the cover of pine trees as I came along the path.

"*Hola*, Juan. And *hola* Canela."

"So, I hear you're taking the goat herder on?" Juan commented as we walked on.

"Pascualet? Yes, well, we're going to give him a go," I replied, rather pleased with myself.

He stopped, turned round, and so did his dog.

"Do you know you and she, are both completely and certifiably mad?"

"What, why? We took him for a trial walk. He was energetic and upset, but why not? Otherwise, he was just fine."

Juan laughed. "He's regarded as unmanageable. They say dogs have intelligences up to the level of a three-year-old human child. And, well, Pascualet has already passed his university entrance exam!"

"Come on," I snickered. "Look, if he's so smart, why won't anyone in the village have him?"

"Because he would soon be running their house!"

"Ahh," I protested as we moved on again. "He might be smart, but he's still a dog."

Juan stopped. "I merely say to you, my friend; don't be all softie, sugary, lovey-dovey over what you are about to do. The locals won't take him because they're afraid of him. No one will admit it, of course, but they are. The Spanish don't train their own dogs, so they wouldn't know the first thing about how to tame this *perro* (dog)."

"Right now, from what I have seen, he's just a frightened, confused dog. Love and discipline are what he needs, in equal measure," I declared boldly for someone who once tried to keep frogspawn in a matchbox.

He stopped again, and we stood four-square to each other across the path. Behind him, as a backdrop, the soaring pinnacle of Sa Muntanya juts into the sky. There should have been claps of thunder and the Berlioz Symphonie Fantastique coming out of the rocks.

Juan bowed. "Salute to you, John, and Kathy. I shake your hand (which he did) while you possess a full set of fingers, which I hope you will have when I see you next. I wish you the very best of luck!" He turned and began walking away.

"Hey wait!" I called after him. "I can walk with you, can't I? After all, I'm just a silly harmless old Englishman adopting a homeless dog!"

3

Javier made the arrangements for us to collect Pascualet. We had wondered why Jorge had taken responsibility to keep the dog since Salvador's death, then our neighbour told us he and Salvador had been close friends.

"I have talked to Jorge, John. Be there at eight. Is okay for you?"

Saturday morning, excited, we were up just after six. At eight, we walked up the steep lane and rang Jorge's doorbell.

"There's no dog barking," Kath noticed.

The garage door opened, and Jorge stepped out, and beckoned for us to follow. We walked to the car park where he had his van.

In we climbed while he explained with gesticulations, that he was taking us to where he had the dog.

Wondering why Pascualet wasn't at Jorge's house, I sat on the back seat which had been covered with a clean soft fluffy throw resembling the hide of a black and white Friesian cow.

The ride in any car out of the village down the narrow road is challenging for anyone with an imaginative bent for disaster. It was new and scary as hell for us but for Jorge, it was as safe and normal as pulling on his boots. I gripped the hard seat-frame of the old Citroën, grateful for a disciplined sphincter. My arms strained to keep me upright whilst up front Kath had securely strapped herself in. Jorge didn't speak; just as well because we couldn't either.

I let go with one hand and tapped Kath's shoulder and shouted in her ear above the engine noise, "Any idea where we're going?"

She shook her head. We were on the road we'd often travelled that drops sharply from the village and then follows the top rim of the valley.

"Where's he got the dog?" I whispered loudly. She shook her head again.

The bends matched the steep scary drop of the road. These follow the contours of the mountainside; in and out you go, as though you're tracing the lines on an Ordnance Survey map in a Dinky toy.

"He's not dozing off, is he?" I shouted in her ear again, looking sideways at him.

The daily tradition was for farmers to meet early morning in the village bars for coffees and brandies to get them going and wake them up, so they don't fall off their tractors. I watched as his eyelids kept dropping. By the side of the car, the line of white concrete blocks, the only thing between us and the sheer drop below, zapped past like a concrete zip. Each looked capable of being nudged from its base, and of rolling and tumbling down the mountainside, demolishing two or three farms on the way. I could see Kath gripping the dashboard with one hand and side handle of the door with the other.

"It will be worth it!" I shouted in her ear again above the engine noise.

Three blood-draining kilometres further down and on, he slowed, greatly to our relief. I shook the chair in front to show life was surviving on the back seat whilst my wife seemed unable to move.

Jorge, without a signal (not that it mattered; there was no one else around), jammed on the brakes and pulled hard off left up a rough dirt track. The little car bounced around and us in it, but Jorge kept the same stoic look on his stubbly face.

I thought to myself, he must get through a car a week at this rate. A shadowy shape emerged through the dusty windscreen rising over bushes, the views misted further by the early air.

"*Mi casita*," he shouted, not taking his eyes off the track. "*Pascualet está aquí!*" My Cottage, Pascualet is here.

Those next few seconds are emblazoned on my memory. As we came through a broken gate and rose further up towards buildings on the rutted track, an old farm appeared with barns, house, sheds, stacks of old wood, rusted old machinery and broken walls.

We pulled up further towards the farmyard and noticed movement above us. The car windows were closed and the engine noisy, so I couldn't hear much beyond the glass, but something already riveted Kath. There, on a length of chain between two posts on top of an earth bank, was a very animated Pascualet jumping up and down and barking aggressively.

Jorge stopped and opened the door "*Tu perro*! *Aquí, en coche!* No move!" He signalled to us. "*Los otros perros son peligrosos.*" There *were* other *perros* dangerous. As further three dogs showed themselves, he put them on separate chains, entered the yard and plodded towards the entrance to the barn. The barking stopped as their tails fell between their legs, and they disappeared into shadow.

Jorge slipped into the barn after them and, in a few seconds, re-emerged. He came back to the car and gestured us out. We thought he said in Spanish that the huge brown dog standing at the entrance of the barn was the father of Pascualet.

"*Muy peligrosos. no toques, no toques.*" Very dangerous. Don't touch, don't touch.

We had no intention of touching any of those dogs or getting close. Kath and I stood well away from the barn. All the dogs had been barking as Jorge's car came up the lane. But once he was out of the car, the only dog left barking was Pascualet. Jorge approached him with a large bucket of dry dog food, but he shied away along the chain. Jorge got closer, grabbed his collar, and released him.

He shouted to us, "*Coche, coche,*" as he gestured to us towards the vehicle.

We got back in the car. He approached with a very distraught dog. Somehow, Jorge bundled him onto the back seat next to me on the fluffy, soft cow blanket. He was hyperventilating and his eyes were wild. Jorge turned the car back down the lane to the road.

I have never seen such a terrified animal up close. Kath glanced back over her seat. Next to me, Pascualet looked much bigger than

I'd thought, and he was panting so fast I thought he was going to faint or have a heart attack. Instinctively, I put my arm around him and drew him to my side. Pascualet let me. I didn't care that his head was as large as mine, and he was close enough to bite half my face off. To reassure him, I held him, not to restrain but to comfort as I talked to him gently, while the car bumped over the hardened ruts. He was breathing so fast and shallow, several breaths a second, or so it seemed, like a machine out of control. The car now swayed along the narrow mountain road and rolled with every bend.

I got the impression that Jorge had had enough of his dead friend's dog and wanted rid of him as soon as he could. Kath glanced back again, rolling her eyes, looking as alarmed by the way Jorge manoeuvred the narrow lane as by the state of the large, crazed dog we'd just adopted. Meanwhile, I hung onto his shivering body as the crest of the village and our new unexpected future loomed closer with every turn.

Along the way, I whispered to him as I stroked his side, "It's okay, boy. You're going to be okay."

4

We'd wanted a little dog, a puppy we could train. Why the hell had we let ourselves be talked into adopting the last shepherd's dog, Pascualet? He came with baggage; a village reputation for being a fighting dog, untrainable and totally loyal to his former owner,

Salvador, who was now dead and gone. If dogs can, he was likely suffering from trauma.

Christmas 2015, a few weeks after taking him in, we realised we might not have done the right thing. Kath became scared of him, and, though I hate to admit it, so did I. It was in his nature to be dominant and once in our house, that's how he acted. If we weren't his Alpha Salvador, then we must be sheep or goats and he must keep us in our place. He hated being in the house. It was terrible to see an animal so distressed, clawing and gouging the concrete around the front door trying to escape. We took it personally and imagined he hated us for keeping him prisoner. We hadn't just taken a well-used dog on; he came with a trailer load of anxiety and angst.

For the first three months, Kath and I became a little flock of goats. We even thought about getting bells to wear round our necks to make him feel more at home. But we weren't on a mountainside; we were inside, a tiny inside, with only a terrace outside. Then he began this strange, intimidating behaviour with Kath. When she came in the front door and greeted him and then turned to put away her keys, he would jump up and touched the back of her neck with his mouth. He also began nipping with his lips at the heels of visitors, those few brave stalwarts who persisted.

Kath and I don't give up easily. We saw the warnings that he would be difficult, but we took him on. The good news was, so far, he'd not bitten us. But we had spent a lot of time corralled in the wardrobe.

This reminds me of the time (true story this believe it or not) I was writing and making films and designing museums. This mini epic was going into a special exhibition. We needed a video of a timber wolf, loose. To get that effect (if you're not out in nature), you have to film against a special background called a 'blue screen'. This enables you to edit the images into a live action scene. Ok, maybe the crew wanted to kill me? Because, for a few too many seconds, I found myself in a small video studio with a young, fully grown timber wolf that came up to my belly button. He was off his chain and without a minder, who needed to heed a sudden call of nature. That was bad enough, but momentarily I had been left alone with a wild wolf! What was worse as I looked at him and he looked at me, he raised his nose to catch a whiff of the ham sandwich the crew gave me as a working lunch, which, being dead smart, I placed behind my back.

The wolf liked ham, apparently. As I pushed myself protectively against the wall, mayonnaise squeezed out of the sandwich, which I was holding out of sight behind my back. The wolf approached and gave me a look like the whole of me was a ham sandwich.

Thankfully, his minder, relieved but not as much as I was, came back and tempted him away with the help of half a raw chicken.

Sorry for that diversion, but it serves to describe how we felt about our new pet, how stupid. In fact, the idea occurred to me the entire village had set us up, well if not *set up*, then taken advantage of.

So, sod it! We thought. We decided to tough it out. He'd get used to us in a little time, surely? But could we get used to him?

He wasn't a large dog, 22 kilos of solid muscle, with a quickly rising response, a bark from hell and a set of gleaming white teeth like a butcher's knife-rack. He was seven years old when we took him on, seven years of having led an almost wild life.

Soon after Pascual came to live with us, Kath and I became friendly with Clara, a Dutch woman who's lived in the village for decades. Because of her close relationship with Salvador, she knew Pascual and was so pleased when we took him on that she even paid for a special insurance policy in case he ever caused an accident or hurt anyone. After all, she knew his sense of independence and lack of training. She wanted us to have a happy life together.

On the many occasions when Kath and Pascual visited Clara at her house it was noticeable that Pascual wouldn't settle there but wanted to leave as soon as he arrived. Clara explained that when she started seeing Salvador and visited him at his house, Pascual would growl at her, almost under his breath. To her amazement Salvador stopped him by simply whispering his name. She believed the dog was jealous of her. Laughing, she recalled a time sitting on the sofa, she and the dog on either side, making a Salvador sandwich.

Clara told Kath that her brother, a vet in Holland, said Pascual was part Belgian Malinois. We looked up the breed and realised that he fit the description like a glove. First bred as herders near the city of Malines in Belgium—hence their name—because of their trainability, they're also used for protection, search and rescue, and bomb and drug detection. Apparently, a Belgian Malinois was on the US SEALS mission to find Osama Bin Laden. Such is their skill and courage that there's a life-sized bronze statue of the breed installed at the Special Operations Force Dog Memorial in Fayetteville, North Carolina, USA, dedicated to all Special Operations dogs.

Mals are squarely built, alert herders, loyal and fearlessly protective with strong territorial instincts. They're known for their strength, stamina and dexterity. That fits our dog. Because they're highly athletic, owners must pen them behind high fences (this made me think of our friend Erik's story about Pascual climbing his chain-link fence to get to his female dog). One website about dog breeds stated they are one of the most proud, intelligent, and hardworking dog breeds in existence. (That's something.) They require extensive training to help minimise any behavioural issues and to keep their mind engaged. (How extensive will be enough with Pascual?) They form an unbreakable bond with their human. (Yes, he was like that with Salvador. So, where would we fit in?) One very interesting character trait of the breed is their aloofness. That explained Pascual's peculiar behaviour around people who approached him; most often he ignored them, showing no interest in their petting, cooing, or being made a fuss of. Their lifespan is twelve to fourteen years. Another website mentioned the Belgian Malinois appears in the *John Wick* movie franchise. Another interesting fact is that they are not recommended for households with children or the elderly due to their strong will and physique. Things were beginning to make sense. Our hands were going to be full.

The stress of those first few weeks didn't end at the front door of our house. Having him on the lead was like wrestling a great white shark and you never knew what might happen next.

We were both in our mid-sixties, having just escaped the jungle that is the cafe business. We tired of the daily battles. He wasn't a pet; just trying to put his lead on was like going into the lion's cage.

Strange how things can work out, though.

Once we rented a village house in Tàrbena, we took our time to decide if this indeed was the place for us, an authentic, working village that felt real and alive. Then, once we had, we began searching for a permanent home, one that we could afford.

We didn't want a tumultuous life; a quiet one would do, especially after my wife's decades of living and owning and running businesses in NYC. You've heard the expression "24/7"? That was our life in a numerical nutshell.

So, dog free at the time, we'd found this great little house, bought it, and fixed it up. We made new friends, mostly immigrants like us, many of whom had been here for years and built their own places. We soon found ourselves absorbed into the local social network and did our bit by hosting and going to parties which came one after the other. But after a while the social whirl became overwhelming and though it was great to make new friends, we realised it wasn't all that we'd come to Tàrbena for.

At our little house, throughout our first year, as one lot of new friends left, another bunch arrived. They were lovely, all of them, but it got crazy, as people began dropping by out of the blue. It was as though we'd never left Kath's cafes in New York City. After a month or two of our new *quiet* life, we were knackered all over again, but this time with a nice tan.

One day, an exhausted Kath, worn out by the constant production of finger food, slumped into a chair, declaring, "It's too much. I can't do it anymore. I wish for a quieter life, please." Oh, my goodness, be careful what you wish for. The Universe was listening.

Kath and I both believe in manifestation, putting out a sincere wish to the Universe. Trouble is, the Universe has a tendency to interpret your desire in ways you didn't contemplate. Ours was covered with brown fur and had fangs.

OUR CHRISTMAS GIFT TO EACH OTHER.

December 2015

Paw Camp

The first week he lived inside, in our house, with us. But he didn't like it, was determined to escape, and spent most of his waking time clawing the front door. We built a barrier in front of it with pieces of furniture. So strong was his resolve to break out, he knocked the barrier aside and got on with digging his tunnel. It was like living in a doggie version of a prisoner of war escape movie. In the end, when he'd worn down his claws, he gave up.

Over the coming weeks, something else made us increasingly anxious; unannounced visitors showing up at our house. In the first few days, when curious friends arrived for impromptu social gatherings and fuss-making of our new dog, Pascual calmly went to each one individually who greeted him with a pet, and a welcome to his new home. All of which he appeared to enjoy. He was a natural charmer and handsome with it.

However, his manner soon changed; he began acting threateningly to the same people, and we didn't know why. His behaviour was unnerving, as though he was returning to his herding ways only with bipeds, not quadrupeds. We considered ways to keep him separated from guests, to keep them at their ease. That wasn't straightforward in a house as large as a cornflakes box, with no doors between rooms. Word got round amongst the socialisers of the village, old friends and new, couples and singles; don't pet their new pet if you want to keep your fingers! Theo and Sue, two friends who adored Pascual, came by a second time with a cast iron sign that said, "Beware of Dog" for our front door. I put it up immediately.

Within a month, we realised we had a serious problem. He'd become very protective of us and our/his home, as I noted in my journal....

Pascual's behaviour yesterday was the most disturbing so far. Kath invited our retired Irish dairy farmer, Kenny, to the house in the afternoon. When the doorbell rang, Pascual shot up the stairs to bark at the stranger at the door. I got him on the lead before I let Kenny in. Just as well. Pascual went savagely for him. Luckily, the chain lead stopped him. Kenny has three dogs and has managed animals since he began working on his family farm when he was eight. Still, the incident shook him despite being a big, powerfully built man. But he had the courage to step inside.

Pascual continued to growl, bark and act aggressively when we went down to the terrace. I kept him on the lead; he definitely had it in for Kenny. I would not risk it. Ken stayed with us for over three hours (he loves to do the blarney) and got used to the dog. It was, after all, a beautiful afternoon, with bright warm sunshine and temperatures in the low 20s Centigrade. His life story unfolded in fascinating chapters. Meanwhile, I clung on to the lead whilst Pascual kept his eyes fixed on the garrulous Irishman.

I needed a toilet break. Kenny and I felt confident enough of Pascual (who by now appeared to have got used to him) to let him off the lead. Left alone with the dog, mellow Kenny petted him and made a fuss. Pascual lunged at his face with his fangs drawn. Luckily, there was no contact. I came out quickly from the terrace loo and grabbed the dog. Kenny didn't hesitate to advise me, "That behaviour must be curbed." Quite right, I thought as our new pet looked intent on tearing him to bits.

The next day I wrote:

Two days later, I did my best to curb his behaviour—I put him in the outdoor loo on the kitchen terrace. He didn't mind going in there, but when he heard the voice of a visitor, he went berserk and charged at the door, trying to get out. In doing so, inadvertently he turned the latch inside locking himself in! We drilled through the lower panel and then reached the latch with a piece of bent wire.

Kath had been confident we could turn him around with ample love and attention, but wisely now realised we couldn't do it on our own. After lunch that day, she delivered a bombshell.

"We either take him for professional dog training or he can't stay with us. We can't live like this, intimidated in our home by our own pet." She was adamant. I didn't put up a fight, anyway, I felt the same. We'd done our very best and got nowhere.

She researched long and hard for a trainer. There weren't many around. But she persisted, as she does, and found one in Javea, a town on the coast. That's quite a long drive from our neck of the woods, but if they'd take us, we'd drive to the ends of the world in order to keep our dog.

2

We got in. On our first day we were anxious about attending the class with Pascual, scared that he would go mental around other dogs. He lunged and barked at every dog we passed on our walks through the village. We expected he'd act just the same during the training class.

Our instructions were to collect with the gaggle of owners and their dogs in a car park outside a McDonald's. Having lost our way, we made it just in time for the 10am start. We'd been worried that the journey to the coast, which takes an hour and a bit, would be unsettling for the dog. He was frightened of travelling in a car. When we arrived and opened the rear side door, it was obvious it had been stressful for him. He'd vomited his breakfast, not on the back seat towel, but on the back seat.

Once there at the car park, the owners decanted themselves and their dogs from their vehicles. What an interesting assortment of animals and humans. We were like the cast of a crazy circus.

David, the trainer, came striding over and introduced himself. Straight away he took Pascual on a little walk close to the other dogs to see how he would react. We expected the worst. But no, David didn't chuck us out. That was a relief as all my life people refused or chucked me out of things: Cubs, school, college, pub, and marriages! And now it may happen to my dog! The trainer must have had a positive impression after the test. It was then we realised we were all newbies, and there together so he could check us and our dogs out. Then he had us get back into our cars with our dogs and follow him. We were in a small convoy, the crazy circus on tour. Before setting off he had announced, "Follow me up the mountain."

It was not much of a mountain, not like where we live. After a few minutes' drive, we pulled over at the designated spot. A separate group of ten owners and their dogs were assembling, people were chatting and their dogs wagging their tails, sniffing happily in their doggie way, saying hello. They had obviously attended earlier lessons and knew the ropes. The class was bigger than we'd expected. I saw chaos and carnage, but Kath was totally gung-ho. "It's gonna be great. This will be the making of him and you and me." I remember thinking, I hope there's a loo on the mountain.

David had us gather at the other side of the road on scrubby land. To each, he gave a little rope choker and showed us where to position it on our dogs. This, he explained, would give us the all-important control. It was intense. And of course, Pascual didn't like it one bit.

With lots of yapping, growling and whining, dogs and owners set off on the dirt trail. What followed over the next three hours was a series of drills and social exercises for dogs and owners. David had us do sensitivity tests combined with essential dog-handling and dog-understanding exercises. I won't list them all. But evidently, it's all about the owner's domination of their dog; not through cruel means, but by understanding how a dog sees the world in which he finds himself. That includes you, his owner, other people, and other animals. If he can, it's in a dog's nature to take control. And with a dog like Pascual, to go further and become the top dog, no second place, top dog or nothing.

In reality, David told us, our dog wants to be led rather than be the top dog. He would prefer to relinquish that status and follow another alpha who would decide for him. Such things were eye opening. My anxiety was evaporating. Both of us (Kath was the watcher for this first session) were relaxed. Pascual easily got into how to walk with a human; to the side, never in front, on a relaxed lead, close to the body, in step, and not wildly dashing about smelling every smell that came on the breeze. Pascual learned quickly and so did I. What he and we learned amazed me that first time, it was a revelation.

With the simple rope choker, it was easy to control Pascual in combination with some very simple but effective actions. One, you communicate your level of anxiety or tension through the lead, so be calm. Two, use sharp pulls on the lead to send a signal that you don't want him to do something along with the command, "Stop that." Three, use that short sharp pull, the stop command and then another sound, "sccchhhhh," a kind of hiss made through pushing air over your tongue and through your teeth. It's just like opening a can of tonic. It astonished me how effective and immediate this was in controlling Pascual in many circumstances!

At home, he told us to feed the dog after we had eaten our meal. And he must be allowed into the house after us. These became small but highly effective signals to who's boss of the house.

David would come and talk to us individually now and then after observing how we had done and to explain the purpose of an exercise. Kath looked on and absorbed everything. He said that herding dogs, such as Pascual, are intelligent animals who feel responsible for those in their "care". He agreed with me that

Pascual's aggressive reactions to our house guests, i.e., nipping the backs of ankles of folks climbing the stairs and lunging at faces when strangers stared him in his eyes, is a behaviour learned because of herding goats and being a shepherd dog. When he nipped at our friend Viv's fingers as she was leaving the terrace a couple of weeks ago, he was upset she was leaving the flock without his permission. When mellow Kenny had felt confident of getting close to Pascual's face and stared directly into his eyes, Pascual didn't see him as a human; he saw a large defiant goat, so lunged at his face, not biting, to give him a disciplinary scare. It worked. David said Pascual has to do most things with his mouth; he doesn't have hands.

After three hours doing many exercises that gave equal attention to each dog and owner up and down rocky tracks and gathered in little sandy clearings, it was time to end the class and return to our cars. I needed the loo and passed the lead to Kathy, who we had now re-joined. I went out of sight and as soon as I had, I heard yelping and barking. It was Pascual. He sounded upset. Emerging from the bushes, he saw me, stopped, and stared as I approached. I was thinking this was simple adoration for his new alpha. With my ego, I would. But no, David explained it was because I had the temerity to leave his flock, and he wanted me back. As we followed up the sandy path, David spoke with us again; he thought Pascual did very well on his first day out.

This was our first session at the Paw Camp. Encouraged, we felt thankful that we may have found the help we desperately needed.

3

For our second class, we set off to cross the 927 metres high (or 3,044 feet) spectacular viewpoint on the way down from Coll de Rates at 8:45am. The Jalon Valley, which we crossed on our way to Javea, was dreamlike in its early morning magnificence as haze and smoke from winter fires mingled in layers close to the bottom of the valley. The sun was rising over the coastal mountain peaks and rays of sun streaked across the sleeping vineyards. Illuminated veils hung low in the air on the sides of the encompassing mountains. Villages on little hills poked through the mist like fairy castles. All was peace and tranquillity this early Sunday morning. That is until we got to Javea and the loads of crazy dogs in need of special training piled into the little car park with their dysfunctional owners.

This time Pascual had travelled well and not been as nervous. After smelling the bag of dog treats Kath packed along with his water and bowl, he was happy to jump into the car.

I was relaxed this visit and could study the owners in the McDonald's car park, the variety of people—old, young, well-off, some not so much, flash cars and scratched cars like ours, all different nationalities—and types of dogs. I watched how the owners related to their dogs and noticed how, in some cases, looked just like them. We're a mixed bunch, but there are some cases of dog and owner where you think the person's never going to manage that dog, for example, the tiny woman and the giant dog. It was the biggest Great Dane that I'd ever seen, the middle-aged lady teeny by comparison. As it must weigh more than her, at that level of simple physics, the woman was at some disadvantage, to say the least. He did what he wanted and simply dragged her along. We thought we had problems.

Then there was the car she arrived in, herself and two dogs, the Great Dane and a big hairy something. The car was about the size of a fiat 500. I think the dog probably weighed more than the car and her together. We stood in awe as she struggled to extricate herself, a dog as large as a baby elephant and the furry one from the rest of the car. How on earth had she got here?

Then there's a lass, maybe early twenties, of slight build, with this tank of a pit bull. She "controlled" the poor animal with an unending series of kicks, shouts, screams, slaps, and thumps. And we were still in the car park. Why the dog hadn't eaten her or bit off her hands, we don't know.

Unlike last Sunday's session in Calpe on the rocky tracks, Dave conducted today's session on flat sandy paths in a sort of recreation area, which included a fenced-in dog exercise compound. Next to this were urban housing developments.

We did the routines, some of them challenging for dogs and owners, on the paths and open spaces and then on a road amongst the houses. David impressed me with the way he used the environment and a few props, like a water bottle and a container of raw minced meat. After two and a half intense hours, the session was over. We gratefully handed over our ten-euro fee.

We were about to leave and noticed the fenced-in dog park. Kath and I looked at each other, then looked at Pascual wagging his tail and feeling pleased with himself. Dare we, for the very first time outside our own house, let Pascual off the lead amongst other dogs? We weren't certain, so we asked David. "Sure, go ahead." Somewhat nervously, we entered the compound. We saw Pascual was of average height compared with the other dogs. There was one enormous dog in there and a few smaller ones. Sure enough, as soon as he was off the lead, this great big mutt came thundering over. We backed against the fence, fearing the worst. By this time Pascual had discovered tennis balls lying ownerless and unclaimed in the grass. It was love at first sight, but how to pick them all up? He had no interest or concern about the large lolloping lumpadog that showed interest in Pascual's very personal space between his back legs where his balls used to hang. (They were there when we adopted him, prior to our having him castrated, hoping he'd be less aggressive. The vet had to remove them because of a post-procedure infection. It didn't change him at all, unfortunately.)

After a while, he tired of running after the tennis balls we'd thrown, making it easy to put his lead back on. We salvaged two tennis balls to take home, we didn't think he would have left otherwise. Then he was as happy as Larry. We returned to the car park and began our journey home.

In the following weeks we went to several other sessions, now able to enjoy them and the extraordinary change in our dog's confidence and ours. We learned how to be the alphas in our home with a few simple actions and routines which worked a dream. So much so that by the month of May, I could write this in my journal….

Pascual and me. My life has changed so much because of him. Each day now I take a longer walk, most often a walk of exploration. We have adventures together. Today was no exception. The adventure is in finding new routes in the wilder, uncultivated areas on the hills and mountainsides beyond the village. I could have done this alone without Dog. But it's so much more enjoyable with a fit dog for company. And what company he is. His past makes him special. Few owners own a retired goat-herding dog. It affects things. Because the police said he must be on a lead in the village after an incident before we adopted him, I'm now taking him out to remoter parts where I can get an idea if there are other people and dogs about. So only when I'm assured, I let him off the lead. The old men of the village in those first days, when we took him on, told Kath and I, "Never let him off the lead or he will be gone, off back into the wild from where he came." When I let him go off the lead on the mountainside, I realised I'd never witnessed joy in an animal before. In that moment of release, he became the epitome of a fit and athletic dog in explosive motion. Seeing him makes my heart glad. He runs, leaps, and jumps up and down the stone walls as though height and gravity mattered not at all. He chases the wind. I've seen him do it in the grass; he stops, sniffs, and runs on. He's poetry in motion. His freedom and the joy of it bless my soul. Though we've had problems over the last three months since we adopted him, we have no regrets. Rather, we feel privileged now to share those magical moments when he defines the meaning of the phrase, "in his element".

Another visit to the Paw Camp. Off we set again, Kath, Pascual, and me for our Sunday dog training school. Pascual is now unconcerned about riding in the car and he was calm as we crossed the mountains and dropped into the Jalon Valley 2000 feet below. We thought we were late but arrived at the meeting point just four minutes after 10am before David and his wife, our trainers, arrived. We never know what form of exercises we as a group will be doing. It came as a surprise to all that we would spend the next two hours in the fenced-in dog compound next to where we do exercises.

In we all went. For reasons known only to him, David had me go in first. "Take off Pascual's lead," he instructed, "and walk to the end and back." Guess he wanted to see how he would react.

The only dogs around were the ones belonging to our group. After a few familiarisation exercises, he asked us all to do something no owner, and certainly no dog, expected. He asked us to let our dogs off their leads all at the same time. I couldn't believe it. I thought there'd be carnage, as some dogs acted fiercely on their leads towards the other animals. The owner of a very scary and very large dog, who regularly attacked other dogs, looked at me as though to say, "Is David crazy?" But David wasn't crazy, and he knows dogs. And that's why we were there. So, tentatively, and nervously, off came the leads. What would happen?

Astonishingly, nothing violent or aggressive. David had us do various exercises with the dogs off their leads. The first was challenging for owner and dog. He placed a small packet of raw minced beef on the grass. Without touching the dog and without leads, we had to walk over to this tasty treat (our Pascual hadn't eaten yet) and walk around it with our dog by our side. The dog must not go to the meat. Pascual sniffed the air, took an interest, but as he looked like he was going to it I shouted, "Stop!" and he turned away. We walked around the tray of meat twice. He stayed with me obediently before returning to our place in the line. I watched as he watched the other dogs intently as they carried out the same exercise. The owners all applauded as each dog walked around the meat with his owner without a leash. This obedience was a revelation to all of us. Everybody and their dogs made it except the little lady owner of the huge Great Dane over whom she still had no control whatsoever. He went straight for the beef and the plastic tray, and it took David to extricate the tray from his enormous jaws. What a brave man. That Great Dane was really thick.

Another exercise, which also scared all of us, was "meet and greet." In this, we had to approach one of the other owners in a neutral space between two lines of owners and dogs and say hello to the dog owner in a friendly manner. The dogs were to remain at our sides unleashed. During the few previous sessions, none of us would have dreamt of doing such a thing. But once again, there was no problem. The morning went on without mishap when David called out to everyone. "Okay, let them all go." There was some trepidation. Pascual, bless his little paws, was good as gold around the other dogs. He even went over to one of them and gave it a sniff. It's obvious that dogs and certainly ours act differently when off the lead.

It was a great success. I thought he was coming on in leaps and bounds. He was good in the car on the journey home and sat quietly beneath the table where we ate a scrumptious pizza at the public swimming pool restaurant in Orba.

4

This was a significant day especially for "*perro* one" in our lives at *Casa sa Rubia* (The Blonde House, the name a previous owner, a blond French hairdresser, gave the house). He was going for a long stay with the dog trainer. For despite the small successes from the training sessions, Pascual had now turned his attention to Kathy, his mission: to subject her to his domination. My wife doesn't take domination from man nor beast lying down or standing up for that matter, so it was time for drastic measures. We called David the trainer for help and told him about Pascual's last jaws on Kath's neck event. Straight off, he invited Pascual to his house to share time with him, his wife, and a gang of other in-training dysfunctional doggies. Relieved, we gladly accepted his offer and the daily price-tag that came with it.

We got him into the car without too much fuss and off we went to the coastal town of Moraira, where David lives with a load of dogs—their own and ones they take on for therapy. The first part of the journey from our village over the mountains and down into the valley was pretty much okay. But three-fifths of the way, perhaps because of the stress of the last couple of days, I started with an ophthalmic migraine. My vision dissolves into something akin to a psychedelic rock show without the music.

What made it worse was that we had to find David's place. The urbanisation in which he lives turned out to be a nightmarish hell of a rabbit warren by the sea. Kath, who was now driving, couldn't navigate alone, especially with the insane American woman's instructions on the GPS once we had entered the labyrinth. We kept going wrong. With an attack, I can't see the real world as an electric storm takes over my brain. Flashing coloured shapes fill my vision, so helping with navigating was impossible. We lost our way. Pascual sensed it and was getting worked up. Would we ever find our way again?

After an hour, my head had cleared to an acceptable level of nausea and functioning, we had stopped shouting at each other, and thankfully we found the address.

Eleven days later, we returned to the next group training session to collect him and receive his school report. As days go, it was a big one for our little family. To be honest, I'd missed him, and I was nervous he'd have moved on and forgotten us, or worse, in his doggie way, given up on us! So, it was with some apprehension we waited as David's van pulled up at the car park where the dogs were let out.

I thought, this is what it must feel like when your child comes home from boarding school for the holidays. The back doors of the van opened, and the dogs piled out. At first, I don't think Pascual recognised us. He was too busy doing what he was being told. But then he recognised us and was all over us—so much so that David asked us to calm down so the dog would. Pascual's excitement seemed a lot to do with the fact that David had his Kong, his squeaky ball that he'd become obsessed with. For a few minutes David had him doing exercises with it, but Pascual did not keep it, as he always did with us. Apparently, though, we thought that him playing with his tennis balls was fun for him. Dave explained that constantly containing them was stressful for him and his relationship with them had become obsessional. It was as though they had taken over from the goats, which were his responsibility to keep under control. Who knew?

Apart from being stressed after our reunion, he was great in class, was now totally okay with the other dogs, on and off the lead, and even walked at my side off the lead.

The training class was good. I don't know why but I thought Pascual might be concerned that he was not coming home with us. At the end, as Kathy was sorting out the car, he focused on one thing only: getting into our car in any way possible. He jumped on the back seat on his own, something he'd not done before. We wanted him in the load area in back, but he would not budge. There was no growling or anything; he just wouldn't move. He travelled all the way home with the safety belt on, so happy and relieved, I swear he was smiling.

To our surprise, when we got back to the village and opened the front door to the house, he ran in. Instead of making a hectic check round, he dashed down the steps to the kitchen and onto the terrace as soon as we'd opened the door. He plunked down on the tiles in the sunshine, closed his eyes, sighed, and went straight to sleep as though saying, "This is my home. This is where I'm staying. I'll be a good boy. Promise, don't worry."

Welcome back, Pascual. Now home feels like home.

March 2016

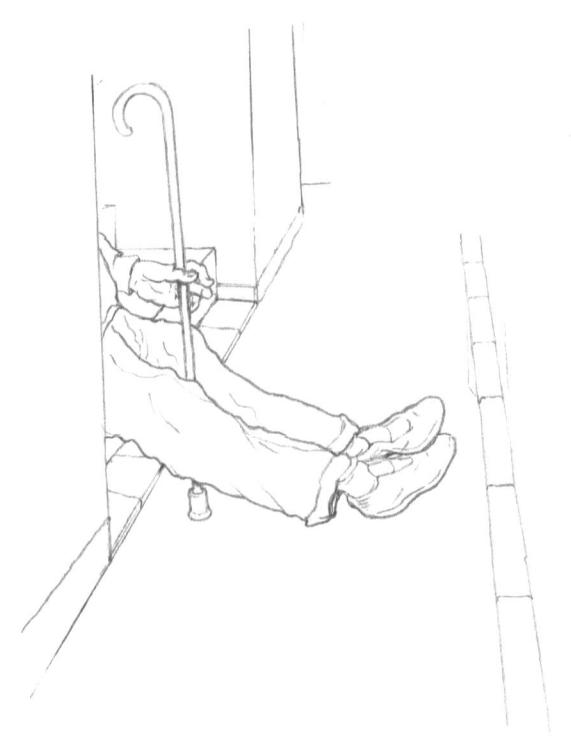

The Village Late May

Summer seeps up the lanes
    shadows sharp as blades
        cut the ways

an old man sits
    asleep on the steps
        hand on his stick

in shadow he bathes
    witness to nothing
        but the rounds of the day

Three Men on a Step
(and Other Meanderings)

The senior people of the *pueblo* have their tribes and routines; they have social groups and preferred bars and cafes. After four years and a bit of residing here, I recognise most of them. Some are friendly and greet you with *buenos días*, or usually *bon día* before 3pm. Up to seven in the evening it's *buenas tardes* (good afternoon), and *buenas noches* (good night) after that. Whatever the time of day, Señor Pelut always says, *ah-díos* when he passed by, which tickled us. We thought it meant goodbye, you know, *adiós*, which many people know means good-bye. But someone told me that it means "to god", "may God go with you", a general greeting here when you pass someone in the street. Others are grumpy and express nothing, and some are amiable. The mature folk are as much a part of the village as the young, and they don't miss a thing.

The gentleman who lives next door to us is ninety-six. Their tall house sits perched on the edge of a cliff (like ours) overlooking the limestone gorge like a lookout post on a castle tower with a view all the way down to the sea. He doesn't wear glasses and perseveres in helping his wife hang out the washing from three wires strung on a metal bracket which hangs on the outside wall of the terrace. That means there's always a chance a favourite tea towel will fall 50 feet below. Fortunately, we're able to retrieve it for them. Though he's stooped and stone-deaf, a retired farmer, he enjoys being outdoors and shuffles along the narrow lanes with his stick, keeping an eye on what's going on. Then, if it's a pleasant day, he lumbers to a spot where he and his *amigos* sit in the winter sun or the summer shade.

I saw him last week, in his baseball cap and cardigan. He was heading towards the school where there are a series of concrete benches, descending step-like against the wall of the school. You have an extraordinary view from our mountains to the sea beyond. Having been born in the village and spent their whole lives here, you might think they would become a little bored or nonchalant about the scene. That's not the case, because every day, every hour, the light changes and with it, the spectacle.

A great rock cliff to the right and an impressive pinnacle of limestone opposite frames the scene. It's crowned with a gaggle of noisy ravens perched on top, carrying on as ravens do. Below where the venerable guys sit is a rocky V that leads to the gorge that was carved by water over eons of time, later sculpted with Moorish stone-walled terraces that gracefully follow the curve of the land like rows of stepped seats in a giant arena. They call it The Balcony. The first time I heard the name the locals bestowed upon this amazing geological feature, I was humbled by how right the name was. It's a theatre of nature if there ever was one.

You can see the coastal town of Albir at the northern limit to the distant southern edge of Benidorm. We delight in watching, during the day, yachts sailing into the bay, cruise and container ships farther out to sea. At night, cruise ships pass along the horizon, slowly and luxuriously; brightly lit up, disco lights flashing. I imagine the parties going on.

There was room for one more on the bench. He made his slow way to it, walking stick in one hand and a square piece of cardboard in the other. Was he going to use it as a sunshade, as I have seen other seniors do? As I walked up from the cemetery below, I saw another chap bearing a similar object. I was curious what they were for. It was warm; perhaps they would be for fanning themselves. But it became obvious; cardboard squares served two purposes—insulation and cushion. Concrete might or might not be cold or hot depending on the season, and it is hard, anytime. And dusty; airborne dust is a fact of life here. The cardboard squares were for sitting on, placed before the men turned and sat. This might stretch a point, but it made me think of just how resourceful the residents are. For centuries, they lived in the back of beyond and had to make a lot of the things they needed. The cardboard cushions were in that tradition.

As well as groups of senior men, there are also cliques of senior ladies. They are friends and enemies too, no doubt with long histories stretching back to when they would have attended the small local school together. Some of the men and women I have heard, rarely, if ever, left the area, even now when travel is so much easier. They didn't need to. It was the tradition here that the men went out to work, whilst the women took care of the home, did the shopping, prepared meals, and brought up the children and cared for their elder parents. It seems so natural, the way people used to live, in community.

As housewives and members of a resident family with relatives also living locally, they had, and still have, most everything they might need right here. And what they don't have, they make themselves as they did in the past. I know that for a fact. At home on the wall of our dining room, we have a small collection of antique locally made items. My favourites are three ancient, handmade brushes exquisitely crafted from esparto grass, native to southern Spain and north Africa.

Besides do-it-yourself, there's a very well stocked, modern general store, which is as much a social centre as a shop. There are two bread shops; a lady has tucked one in a converted front room of her house. She sells bread brought up the hill daily in a speedy van from a bakery in the town down the mountain.

At the other end of the village, and closest to us, is an old-fashioned bakery with a cosy shop at the front and a wood-burning oven in the back that re-opened recently. It's on the corner of a lane that drops into a steep valley. Its name *Forn de Pà* used to be hand-painted in plain black letters on the wall above the door. The new owner replaced it with a colourful mural with its new name, *Can Ran*. The young baker bakes in the middle of the night and, during the day, drives a tractor. I don't know what he does for sleep. When I step inside, time disappears like yesterday's stale bread. It could be twenty, forty, sixty years ago.

In front of you is a glass case presenting the day's *coca*, a thick, yeasty crust topped with concentrated tomato sauce and an assortment of spicy sausages and charcuterie. If you come early enough, you'll see empanadas of the day, usually filled with tuna, vegetables, and the same sauce. They are delightful for your *desayuno* (breakfast) especially when you pop in to take a couple home after your early-morning walk. What could be nicer?

Behind the counter is the amiable lady who serves the customers, continuing the stream of conversation with each. It's an exchange I imagine must stretch back over generations. Even if you aren't buying bread or something more savoury, the aroma wafting through the door is satisfying enough.

I walk past two or three times a week with my dog at the start of our morning walk. There's always animated chatter inside. Though I listen as we pass, I have yet to understand a single word. The residents address each other in their own special hybrid language, inaccessible to us. But the lady is gracious to me when I'm there to buy and speaks in *Castellano*.

The conversation and exchange of news must be as important as the daily bread. I love to go for a loaf to make the ever-popular *tostada con tomate*. It's a baguette sliced in half lengthwise, toasted, drizzled with the local olive oil, and spread with grated fresh tomato. It's the Spanish equivalent of butter and marmalade on toast. At first, I was apprehensive about making an idiot of myself, and coming home with a sack of flour instead of a stick of bread.

The Last Shepherd's Dog

But I developed a means to communicate using the words I know and body language.

It's a minimal exchange; the lady serving reaches back to the shelves of variations of fresh-baked golden fat crusty sticks, taking one from the wooden shelves where that morning's baked goods await their fate. You select the size of the stick by pointing. And when it comes to paying, as most things there cost less than a euro, you slap a one-euro coin down on the glass-topped counter. You watch her twist a delicate sheet of wrapping paper too small to enclose the entire golden beauty but big enough to make a well-practiced twirl and a small but ingenious knot to keep your sweaty, dog-walked hand off the fresh loaf. Then she slides your change across the glass. After years in New York City, I can't get used to getting change for anything!

Other times, when you are in the vicinity, the smell of

fresh baked bread wafting through the door is enough to make your thoughts turn to breakfast. The timbre of the chat emanating through the open door caught on a spring morning re-assures you that the village you have chosen to spend the rest of your life in is alive and kicking.

If that morning you lust for something fancier, try the patisserie on the edge of the village. It's a bit showier with mirrors and lots of glass and a baking area which you can look into through a glass wall. Definitely not traditional. We wonder if the villagers will take to it. Maybe they hope to get passing trade as it is on the mountain road; we shall see. I wouldn't count my *vol-au-vents* quite yet.

On fine days, we are beginning to see cyclists in shiny spandex and helmets pulling up just outside. They're like visitors from outer space who have travelled from the farthest reaches of the universe, because three thousand light years ago they fancied cream-filled meringues and a cheese, ham, and tomato baguette, and so they had their mission. Good job the café was open when they got here.

There's a magical *farmacia* (pharmacy) as well. I call it so because it has one of the most extraordinary locations on the planet for a chemist. It occupies a small number of rooms crammed on the ground floor of one of the last buildings at the southeast side of the village. The street hangs onto a strip of land set on the rim of a precipitous valley, like teeth in an uneven smile. It has to be the most beautiful establishment of its kind anywhere.

I swear, the act of going there, in that setting, with the cheery smiling welcome, feels like a burst of life-giving sunshine when you enter. The experience is a tonic in itself. She happily answers any question you may have about prescriptions or symptoms. But overall, it is her ringing laughter that's the cure-all. Especially after years living in New York City, reluctantly visiting the pharmacy where "ching, ching, ching" and "Next!" was all you heard.

Below the *farmacia* is the school playground, and beyond that a huge void of air, haunted by waifs and strays of misty wannabe clouds and a pair of eagles, posses of ravens and chattering choughs and the occasional fire-watching helicopter.

As a grandiose backdrop to this theatre of air, the Bernia Mountain soars up from the coastal plain like a giant witness. It's a vista so impressive, so beautiful it makes you feel better just going there and seeing it. Sometimes as I stand outside waiting my turn, breathing the most bracing, stimulating fresh air straight from the Mediterranean, I feel better and wonder why I'm there, because I feel so alive.

Once a week the fresh fish shop opens, all white tiles and ice. A lady in a rubber apron and matching boots, along with her husband as rosy faced as she, brings the fish up from the coast in a white van. I fancy she just stepped off a fishing boat that morning having caught the fish herself.

On a parallel lane is a hairdresser, popular with the local ladies and located in the front street-level room of an old house.

As for food, the village folk grow a lot of fruit and veg to feed themselves. Most families have their own parcels of land even now, as it's still very much a farming community. There's a constant cornucopia of seasonal crops: artichokes, onions the size of cannonballs, garlic, apples, oranges, lemons, cherries, almonds, melons, squash, persimmons, and avocados. Nísperos, or loquats, are grown under massive plastic tents scattered throughout the hilly landscape. And there are grapes for making homemade wine and olive oil from the olives grown everywhere which are pressed in the next village in the autumn. Receiving another bucketful of lemons can be almost an embarrassment.

We can buy fruit and vegetables at the small open market in the square on Thursday mornings. The handsome man who runs the green grocery stall has many lady fans. He's the equivalent of a visiting rock star, only he holds a cucumber rather than a microphone. I've seen ladies squeezing his tomatoes and squashes and fondling his eggplants for longer periods of time than required.

The Doctor's surgery and village clinic here are very important, especially as the population is ageing. I see the doctor (or nurse) with trust in my heart because my conversational Spanish is, shall we say, pathetic? And emerge with a prescription for what? I'm never quite sure! But as with the *farmacia*, the people who see you and treat you are warm and sincere. Going to see the doctor in the village clinic is akin to looking forward to seeing an old friend. We are so very fortunate, and as with the *farmacia*, there are no parking problems as both places are under five minutes' walk away.

Back to those ladies at the vegetable stall, I have some favourites. There's one who wears a knitted or crocheted hat, in the summer when it's boiling and winter when it's not. Once she had on a kind of pink bucket. Then there's a small-of-stature lady in her nineties, smiling and gadding about. She ought to wear a hat too, as at her great age, she hasn't much hair and she might get a head cold or a skull tan.

A venerable lady whom I call with all respect, Mrs Sausage, is a senior of regard and confident demeanour. She's the matriarch of the family that owns and runs the village sausage factory and the bar on the plaza. Mrs S, whilst only about four feet tall, carries a parasol in the summer and looks as if butter wouldn't melt in her mouth. She's as sharp as a tack. She adds up your items on a scrap of paper with a stub of a pencil that has added up vast amounts since last sharpened.

At no detriment to her, I must admit to being nervous. When I enter the shop, she wipes the floor with me for being so inept and unable (by now after years of *Castellano* Spanish classes) to speak a syllable of the *Valenciano* spoken here. She considers it a sin, I am sure, and a disrespect to the community. I notice this from her withering expression as she goes silent in frustration with me and gives me my change to get me out of the shop.

She sells home-made dried sausages of various flavours and sizes made by her son, and wonderful wine at very reasonable prices. Shame, I would love to be a regular customer. Truth is, I don't go in as much as I would like to; I don't wish to be metaphorically smacked round the face with a wild boar sausage by Mrs S, always coiffured and dressed to go out to dinner.

There's another lady, who, whatever the weather (and being up a mountain, it is changeable), who again is ever immaculate. She wears high heels and a large handbag draped on her arm, even in a storm. She, according to the rumour mill, is from an aristocratic background. I can believe that, as I feel like bowing when I see her.

But my favourite ladies are the ones I refer to as the Walkie-Talkies. I'm recognising the locals as I wander about with my dog on our morning exercise walks; it's then I see these amazing women and have come to admire them.

Pascual and I take early morning walks. Often our route takes us down the main road to a lane up the mountain. Without a doubt, I shall see them on the road, three, sometimes four, always coming up the other side of the pavement. They chat away, no matter what the weather or temperature, up and down they go, chat, walk, chat. The road has no shoulder and is dangerous with blind bends, so they walk in line. One is tall, another is of medium height and the other is smaller. How they manage conversations in such a linear fashion whilst moving is hard to figure; I think they must pass messages along, from front to back, and then reverse. I yell greetings to them from across the road, while the dogs bark their heads off as my dog and their dog hate each other.

The men love to chat too. Like the ladies, I look at them and see a lifetime of history written in the wrinkles on their faces, their knobbly, brown-skinned, muscled hands, and the twinkles in their watchful eyes.

One morning, though blowy and cold, was also bright. The men know where the best outdoor places are for sitting throughout the seasons, where there will be pools of intense, warm sunlight and shelter from the wind.

We were just coming home from our walk, having shouted my greeting to the ladies. The three old chaps, all white of hair that I see regularly, weren't walking; they were sitting one above the other on a house staircase (in New York City, it's called a stoop), in a little square close to the school. I said, "*Buenos días,*" to them and doffed my hat. "Good day," they spoke in unison, smiling as one. That was a first, believe me, but I know they were addressing Pascual.

As we passed in front of them, the chap on the bottom step called him over for a dose of fuss and attention, a flurry of browned hands stroking and petting him.

Pascualet's as local as they are, is a part of their lives and memories and always will be, for before we adopted him after his owner passed away, he was Salvador's dog, the last shepherd's dog.

Now, he's become "old" dog. Come to think of it, I'm an old dog too. I wonder if there'll be a spare step for my dog and me.

June 2016

Shopping for News

There's one shop in our little village. A miniature supermarket, which provides for the needs of the five hundred plus year-round residents. During the summer fiestas when the population doubles, they do a wonderful job keeping everyone well-supplied and happy.

Just when you think, "I'd better go down the mountain (to civilisation) to purchase something," you check the local shop instead and find what you require hidden behind boxes of matches and bottles of bleach. You make the effort to pop into the shop in the hope what you need is there, because you honestly don't want to drive all that way down the mountain if you can get it here.

When in the village store, you're not actually in a shop as such but a social centre. I swear the locals dress up to go. Visiting it is an event. Fran, the man whose place it is, is an attraction in himself. It's worth going to buy a kilo of fresh sausages even if you're a vegetarian because he sings as he waves his knives about (only behind the butcher counter, don't worry). It's a free show, especially when sometimes the most exciting thing outside is watching last night's empty Coke can roll around the square. Inside, on the other hand, is like being in the brain of the community and the heart of the family. Most times a visit turns into an expedition, and an unplanned and unscheduled social adventure.

My wife and I lived the first twelve years of our marriage in New York City. Millions of humans are crammed together, none of whom want to talk to you. Here, you will die of curses if you don't offer a hello and enquire into a person's well-being when you bump into them. And it's sincere, wonderful. Life is meant to be amongst people. The trouble is, it's a bit hard to proceed from A to B in the village without a backpack of survival rations as it takes so long.

In New York, say you wanted to go to the chemists. You'd arrive quickly and return more quickly, and no one would even look you in the eye—unless they were threatening you with a gun. Here, you call in to the *farmacia* and by the time you finish the errand, the village will certainly know your current ailments and personal and family medical history, dating back centuries.

Although the shop is only about three hundred metres away, along Calle San Antonio, round the bend to the right where Noah the bouncy dog on a balcony barks, up the street and into the *Plaça*, there will be, guaranteed, social encounters of the sticky kind. Entanglements unforeseen will stop you in your tracks and glue you to the spot, sometimes for weeks.

The thing that gets me is that as an immigrant with four years of studying the Spanish language and yet only about ten words remembered (four of which are hello, goodbye, red, and wine), you get involved not only with English-speaking incomers like yourself but with locals.

You know when you watch ants climbing a wall; they all bump heads and exchange information. It's the same here; communication and cementation of the community. Someone at the other end of the village might sneeze, but blessings continue across the rooftops.

That's why when you go to the shop, you'd better take provisions with you!

July 2016

A Tad Less

Like a tear drying out on a face, our charming mountain stream has, after several months, stopped flowing.

Following three years of unremitting drought, out of the sky in the winter arrived salvation, a deluge of titanic proportions. One rainstorm brought sixteen days of continual rain, then we had snow and hail, followed by more intense thunderstorms and manic downpours. It was wonderful, if a little wet.

The locals at first bathed in the showers with clothes on, arms to the heavens, thanking God. They wallowed in it, and dashed about in squealing bliss, as trillions of tears of joy and optimism fell to earth.

The downside was the dry landscape fell to bits and was washing away. Mudslides appeared, trees and power lines toppled, while paths turned to rivers and streams to torrents.

As the deluge proceeded unabated, in the village bars it wasn't long before the celebrations turned to concern and then anxiety, as if the entire mountain could slide into the sea. People hoped the torrent would stop, whilst the more devout saw it as an Act of God and considered building a family ark.

Meanwhile, the frogs who live in the open storage tank on our neighbour's land were delighted. The cistern had filled to the brim, and they were partying like crazy. The future of the frog tribe steadily brightened as sheets of rain fell non-stop from the dark skies, filling the natural underground aquifers.

After several weeks of wet weather, experienced residents announced there was abundant water stored for two to three years' reserve. Though tremendous damage had been done, the deluge was a much-needed miracle, because even the resilient olive trees were showing stress.

The frogs overheard the falling rain and their instincts kicked in. Thoughts of survival turned from deep sleep under the clay to getting together and making tadpoles. Local villagers also noticed the flood as water gushed through terrace walls, into their houses and engulfed their fields. The frogs, meanwhile, swam joyfully in the liquid bounty and began bonking other frogs as though there was no tomorrow.

Across from our little house, there is a steep mountainside, and carved into it a rocky watercourse, known in Spain as a *barranco*. Since we moved in, it remained dry as dust. I used to stand and marvel at how long it must have taken to be carved out of the rock, and how long it took to shape the rocks into channels, pockets, and pools. I could hardly imagine the time it must have taken for flowing water, which rarely flows, to sculpt it and the surrounding cliffs. After several days of downpour, an amazing thing happened.

There was a sound, a sort of roaring. I could hear it even through the rain-spattered windows. We opened one to investigate the source of this great noise and didn't have far to look; the *barranco* had exploded into life. A white water rapid of fantastic energy and fury had materialised.

Here was the hammer and the chisel that had sculpted the rock. It might only happen once in a cloud-hung moon, but its running force robbed atoms in their gazillions from the limestone.

Down the mountain, water rushed until it reached the head of our valley where it gouged out a hole before rushing on again and disappearing underground into a stone-lined drain built by the Moors.

Such was its ferocity that it was risky to get too close. One slip as the waters washed over your feet, and down you would go, green slime beneath you lubricating your slide down and into the wide-open concrete mouth carried into the subterranean drain, burbling, yelling, gasping as the earth swallowed you up. No, we stayed safe up on our terrace as, for days, the rapid below roared angrily.

Meanwhile, pregnant frogs and their suitors were making preparations. When the rain stopped and the rapids became streams of pure liquid crystal, they left their tank and explored the surrounding campo, looking for tadpole nurseries. How they did it is a mystery, but, sure enough, they found the beautiful little pool the rapid had carved out.

One day, after the memories of the rains were themselves waning, I noticed another unusual noise; the voices, screams, and laughter of eager youngsters climbing down the *barranco*, which had now become a lovely stream worthy of a TV advert for shampoo. Would it remain a welcome feature in the landscape forever?

Ok, kids love water, splish-splash. But they weren't splish-splashing; they'd discovered life. The youngest children made the discovery first. They'd come down to the head of the valley to watch the water falling over an edge and down into the drain. I was worried that they could slip and disappear. After they'd gone, I went down to look for myself to see if there was any way of making the area less dangerous.

What I realised was that the children had discovered the tadpoles, hundreds of them, swimming about in the clear water of the pool. I bet those kids, young as they were, hadn't seen tadpoles before because of the years of drought. Off they rushed to tell their parents and friends, who arrived carrying jars and bottles intending to adopt the taddies.

The kids were full of wonder, and it was fortunate they did not empty the pool of its new residents. In the days that followed, the still tumbling stream and pool beneath became a draw for children and adults alike. Only a week ago, we caught sight of a family group, kids and grown-ups, visitors I think, having a family picnic down there around the pool, as the last bemused tadpoles, now frog adolescents, looked up at rippling faces of enchanted children and city worn adults. Here was Nature, risen from the dust and dry bone stone, a veritable miracle.

Just as we thought the campo would come alive, jumping with the frogs and toads of the storm, two calamities occurred.

The surge that fed clear water into the pool ran lower and lower each day as the mountain aquifers reached their water-shed but then surprisingly flowed with force again, but there had been no more rain. The question was, where was the extra water coming from and why was it not clear, but cloudy?

Had there been a cloudburst somewhere in the mountains? No, the sky had remained clear and blue. Wherever the cloudy water was coming from, it continued to flow for several hours, and it worried us. We didn't know for a fact, but it appeared someone up the mountain was emptying or had released thousands and thousands of gallons of some dodgy liquid into the streambed. We worried about the lives of the few remaining tads. Then, as quickly as it started, it stopped. But what about the tiny denizens of the deep?

The next day, on our morning walk, Pascual and I peered into the pool, which was clear once more. Would there be any survivors? To my amazement, the few tadpole teenagers had managed to survive what looked like chemical warfare.

The second and inevitable calamity occurred two days ago; the natural stream overnight had dried up altogether and the little pool was but a greening puddle as the Spanish sun sucked the life out of it. The stream which fed it had once again turned back to dust. Gone was the white water rapid, which had flowed with such legendary ferocity. A band of dry white cracked mud was all that showed its storm-fed course. How quickly the sun here can turn *lush* to *desert*!

This morning, in the course of writing this, I left my lap-top and went down to see if the pool was still there. It was, just. What remains is a puddle of stagnant water, lots of flies and one junior trainer shoe covered in dry slime and yet, much to my surprise, two tadpoles. Will they make it now to maturity? I have to doubt it.

I'm not a religious person, but I pray there is a heaven for all those innocent tadpoles for whom time ran out like the water that sustained them. I hope they're in a crystal pool swimming for eternity, never ageing, always happy and forever young.

One thing I do know now for a fact, based on a few years' experience of living here; the day will come and the rain will fall, definite. The frogs and toads know. They bet their lives on it.

February 2017

Steel Mules

Life in this village feels sometimes like living in a circus of danger and risk. Even today, there is a work segregation regarding agriculture. The wives of the farmers run the home, bring up the children, and look after the elders whilst the men go out and work on the land.

Before mechanisation, donkeys and mules did the heavy work. When tractors became available and affordable, machines took over from the mules. However, as hay and straw gave way to diesel, the old habitual way of life continued.

To an outsider, if you study the way the men work with their tractors today, the relationship between farmer and mule/machine doesn't seem to have changed that much. The first design of tractors reflects that.

Older tractors are fifty years of age and come in two connected parts. At the front is the engine, big drive wheels and controls.

It hauls a two-wheeled trailer with a hard box seat for the driver with tools and food and drink inside, depending on how far that day's work from the village is. An articulated arm connects the two pieces, the front and the towed part.

The engine has a coupling to the various tools attached between the engine and the driver. Handlebars manage the steering and hold the primary controls, like on a motorbike. There's no power-steering wheel.

You steer a ton of dumb power with attitude, with the muscles in your hands, arms, and legs. Imagine trying that with a hangover. No wonder the farmers start the day with a strong coffee and a shot of brandy. I'd need a large Valium and trauma nurse.

If you stand back and take the whole thing in, it's easy to see a mule up front, with a man holding the reins, or walking by the side and cart behind.

To rotovate his patch, the driver removes the trailer and walks behind the engine, controlling the front part with the handlebars.

I watched a local chap rotovating his land the other day. This grumbling machine, flashing rotating knives beneath it and kicking up dust like a monster, outweighed the man by at least four times. He was at the back, hanging onto the handlebars, trying to keep it and himself vertical. Talk about Zen! It's not the time to let your mind wander to something like last night's row with the wife. Sliced salami comes to mind.

Some mules and donkeys could be difficult to work with but working with a steel mule looks downright suicidal to me, especially in this landscape.

Even more dangerous to my eye, was another machine, a smaller version. Seeing it for the first time with Pablo, a neighbour and its handler, one late summer afternoon, I witnessed something I shall never forget.

Where we live is on the rim of a steep gorge, which drops away below us. The early settlers built ours and other houses on a limestone cliff. Probably, because of several freshwater springs below.

Centuries ago, the Moors tamed the land beneath and above on the broad mountainside, levelling it into stepped terraces and small fields called *bancales*. To reach them at this side of the village, you descend one of two very steep paths, both of which today are covered in fractured and uneven concrete. You have to be most careful going up and down on foot, never mind with a load behind you.

I know the chap who appeared with the tilling machine at the top of the track opposite. I said to myself, "He's not going to take that thing down there without help, is he?"

I know that the *hombre* I'm talking about is big in the village church. Maybe he did have Someone helping him, or a team of guardian angels watching his every step. He was going to need them. I honestly couldn't believe it.

Me—I was sitting comfortably, post-lunch, on our sun-warmed kitchen terrace with an all-too-graphic view of the broken track below him. I'm ashamed to say I didn't dash out to offer my help, but I did want to shout, "DON'T DO IT!" Anyway, I knew he would not have accepted my offer as I have often discovered. The local men are independent and self-reliant that way.

Many of the locals, especially the men, have inherited land and now have two lives rolled into one. They might be a village baker but also a farmer and landowner.

This chap, middle-aged and fit, has a plot on a small field below our *casa*. That's where he'll be going, I thought, to use the machine to dig it up. But how's he going to get it down there?

I watched, glued to what unfolded. He stood for a moment on the cusp of the track at the very top. Then he moved decisively, turning with his back to the track falling away into the abyss. He reminded me of a high-board diver about to launch into space. Everything slowed in that moment. He wouldn't do it, surely? But he did. Reaching backwards without looking, his right leg and foot felt below for the first step. Above him the machine tilted as he took his first step. Then it followed him. He took the whole weight on his arms; it must be at least three times his weight. But he held it steady and sure. Carefully, like a ballet dancer with a small truck in tow, he took another step backwards. Then another, small and sure. Now possessed by gravity, the truck followed him, stalking like a leopard, step for step, sure of a kill. The man remained straight armed, changing his angle as he leant in towards it, putting all his weight against it through his arms, holding the handles. Below, sunlight caught the flashes of revolving blades. God Almighty, I couldn't watch.

When I came back from my first quick toilet break, he'd advanced about three meters and still, as far as I could see, was in one piece. He reminded me of a circus act; a cross between tightrope walker, sans pole, a sword swallower, and a knife thrower, all rolled up and diced in one.

Step by careful step, he continued the descent, without looking, just feeling with his feet, each step thoughtful, sensitively taken, a man on a high wire in a blindfold. Meanwhile, holding *muchos* kilos of sharp-edged steel above his waist height. slowly, slowly, with each sensitive step, he continued his steep and fractured descent. One slip, one catch on the edge of broken concrete, one tilt of a slab of broken stuff, one slip on the loose rubble, which rolled, cascading below as it was displaced; one misstep, and the Church would need another candle carrier.

As I watched rivetted, I thought about bravery, I thought about stupidity, I thought about courage, I thought about madness. I thought about horrendous injury! I thought about farming these arid rocky dangerous cliffs, alone in your open-topped cage-less tractor literally on the edge every day.

Unexpectedly, I felt tears well up, misting over the extraordinary scene, one man silent, alone, but for one flabbergasted watcher. It took him at least fifteen minutes to get to the bottom of the track where the gradient returns to something a little less suicidal. All that time he hadn't been able to rest his arms or his concentration. In all that time I felt like I hadn't taken a breath. *I* was the one who was knackered!

He made it of course; he wouldn't have done it if he couldn't have. He hadn't taken a wrong step all that way. I couldn't let my mind wander to how terrible a misstep would be. When he got to the more level bottom, he turned the machine round and started up the engine. It coughed into smoky life of old cogs and black worn-out oil, as though waking from a dream by the sound of it.

I went to the fence and looked down on him. He saw me. I blew in the air, "phew" and rolled my eyes heavenwards. "I don't believe what you just did!" I mouthed in English. He laughed and shrugged his shoulders. He knew what I was saying. *"No pasa nada."* It's nothing." It was all in a day's work.

I sat out as long as he was down there, the engine churning and rumbling, and the blades clattering loose the rocks in the rocky soil. The plume of dust raised I could see rising above trees meant he was ok. I knew the plot, it belonged to someone else.

There were several others already planted from earlier; maybe one was his. Until this point, I had never noticed them. I would now.

Pascual came out to remind me it was his dog walk time. Returning to the *casa* an hour later, the shadows in the street had grown longer and darker, and the street and valley below were quiet. The engine noise had gone, the darkening valley had fallen silent.

Later, as I felt my wife drift off to sleep beside me, I thought about what I'd witnessed and wondered if I'd dreamt it.

Next morning, once again ready to go up and off into the campo with Pascual, as I turned the key in the door, I saw something outside through the frosted door. It looked like a bag or a parcel. The dog went straight out for a sniff. Pulling him back, I looked in; it was full of vegetables—potatoes, onions, and tangles of garlic. As I looked in at this produce, I felt that wave of emotion come back.

I knew what it was about now, something which I had not felt since we'd arrived. For the people of the village who had lived their lives here, people who had worked their land in the hard and unforgiving landscape, as had countless generations before. They who might be the last, older men and women, still working because they are the last, their kids gone off to the hungry cities below.

I didn't know what the Spanish word was for the one that had formed in my mind yesterday. Now, it shone like a medal in my mind. I looked up to the village and the land around and beyond. *Respeto* it said, respect. At that moment life here and the everyday, all around became richer and more meaningful.

May 2017

Dog Blankets

Bar L'Angeles is a small traditional bar with no outside space, except at fiestas when the owner commandeers the narrow street outside for tables and chairs. Inside, she packs the furniture together and the wall-mounted TV, like a blood-shot eye with a persistent twitch, is always on and always loud.

The Spanish are a noisy lot. Come to think of it, in twelve years of being here I've never heard a whisper. Even if nobody is paying attention, the smaller the space and the more people there are, the volume goes up and up. I've begun to wonder if they're all deaf. I mean, I'm deaf and my wife shouts at me all the time.

Back to this old special bar. A sport, pastime and relief from anything audio in the bar is to mentally shut out the surrounding noise and follow the TV News in the reflection in the mirrored pillar which stands in the middle and try to follow the Spanish captions in reverse. Just for fun, it's especially good for the linguistically challenged.

However, the effect of the volume of sound from the television, reflected off the tiled floor, walls, ceiling and mirrored bar, has a reciprocal effect on the customers. Some of whom might be wanting a little peace and quiet.

The quietest place there I discovered is the toilet. But even in this private little space you are not cut-off from the audio life of the bar. It has a window into the storeroom next to the kitchen, so whilst you meditate you can listen to the kitchen staff shouting at each other.

Never mind the noise though. That's the way Spanish people like it; noise in this country means *life*.

Noisy it might be but it's a great spot to meet friends. It's a genuinely welcoming place and that feeling is infectious. It's friendly, reliable and accepting of outsiders who, like us, not only enjoy, but who are grateful for the affordable *Menú del Día*.

At the time of writing, you could have had a home-cooked three-course meal and half a bottle of vino for under nine euros, whether you have a mule outside or not. *Menu Del Día*, was originally created country-wide for working people during General Franco's time, which ended in 1975. It still exists in some places like Bar L' Angeles, *and* the proprietor doesn't mind if you shout at her to order it.

Partly because of the affordable food and drink, it's a great place to meet your pals.

There are daily regulars, locals who've lived here all their lives and some outsiders, redoubtable individuals, the expats, *extranjeros*, who moved here decades before and who have also spent a large chunk of their life polishing the same stools at the bar.

They are very regular, regular as clockwork. At different times during the day, different ones arrive. Alone or with company, they come in, nod to all, and take up their place at the bar or a table, or, if just for a glass of something, they might stand. A small group of farmers, our neighbours, regularly come in after work and before dinner to play cards, a time to get together and wind down. Whatever though, they all come in for a nice shout. Lunch arrives fresh from the kitchen preceded by the laying of paper tablecloths on the table, if you're eating.

What I love most about Maria's is the dottiness of the incumbent Brit regulars, whom I hope over more time to emulate. Tàrbena does have something of a reputation for, how shall I put this, a certain eccentricity. Well, the barmy old Brits have taken this to heart and do their bit.

In fact, the bar is a sort of daily Crazy Comedy Show with laughter the most common sound. As the wine and spirits flow, the verbal intercourse becomes more erratic, louder and bizarre.

I don't want to be all arty-farty here, but sometimes it strikes me as being absolutely surreal, from where reality is elsewhere beyond the swinging bead curtain at the door, outside, with the flies and summer tourists put off by the raucousness from inside. It can be fabulously barmy, like the conversation of last week I had with a great pal and senior Brit denizen of the village, the lovely, retired nurse, Diane. She's pushing her eighties and is as tough as ball-bearings. She's seen it all.

She was one of the first people we met when we let down our anchor in the village. She's also probably the happiest person I've ever met. A regular at lunchtime, the bar is in several ways a staple of her life. She's about to have a senior birthday. I love her to death. We never have a quiet chat because we are both a little deaf, so read the following as a sort of shouting match.

"Hola, Diane, how are you today. It's almost your birthday, isn't it?"

"I'm busy." She seemed a little distracted. Not interested in her birthday.

"What with?"

"Dog blankets."

"What?"

"Dog blankets… I'm making them."

"Who for?"

"Dogs, of course."

"Oh."

"I'm making them."

"I see. Are you knitting them?"

"Dog blankets?"

"Dog blankets, ah. What sort if not knitted, crocheted then? For small or large dogs?"

"Yes, I make them."

"Do the dogs commission them?"

"No, course not, the owners. They like them."

"Who the dogs?"

"Yes, and the owners. From quilts."

"From what?"

"Quilts, I cut them up."

"For the dog. Whose quilts?"

"Yes, dog blankets."

"Oh."

"Did I tell you I'm making them?"

"Yes, you did."

"Who made the quilts?"

"I did, but now I make…"

"Dog blankets, I know."

"How did you know?"

"I heard."

"Word's got round then?"

"Yes."

"About the dog blankets?"

"Yes."

"Rumours spread quick in this village." She looked round suspiciously.

I leaned toward her. "Can't keep anything quiet, especially in here."

"Especially about my dog blankets. They're for dogs only, you understand. And if you write about this, I'll kill you!"

I don't think I'll be going in today, because the rumour is that she was once a spy in North Africa at the end of the war.

But then again, I could always fib and say I hadn't heard her.

June 2017

Market Mornings

Before dawn
an alarm
summons the *verduras* man
to his van

Then up the wiggly windy
as light behind climbs

and lettuces sleep
in a tremulous heap
Still there
the village square
clock in the tower
makes a moon of the hour

Clatter of crates
onions, and grapes
tomatoes, pimientos
patatas, manzanas

Next stalls
the man with fish in a van
and the flowering bush man
dressed all black in a flat black cap

Behind the shutters
the Priest wakes
a yawn-dog barks
day breaks

Water boils in the bar,
grounds scald
brandies pour
as the tower calls the hour once again

John Sunderland

As apples bright faced
find their place
in the browned hand
of a man of significant age

And ladies in knee stockings
squeeze here, squeeze there
a tomato, a pear
in the brightening square

Whilst the African man as black as Sudan
with watches and shades
makes a bed of the church stones by the rail
dreaming of a bright morning and multiple sales

June 2017

Silla Season or the Wrong End of the Stick

Just when you think you're getting somewhere with your Spanish communication skills, an incident comes along that shows you're not doing as well as you thought. That happened to me one day in our village. I share it with you to illustrate how very easy it is to mis-communicate and almost get your nose broken.

Our Spanish neighbour was clearing out his large basement. By 8:30 am, with the help of another local man, he'd already stacked his trailer with old furniture and bits and bobs destined for their *casita*, a cottage in the *campo*.

Our neighbour's a smashing chap and one with whom we've worked hard to cultivate a friendly and trusting relationship.

As my dog and I set off for our morning walk, we saw he'd left a rather handsome rocking chair at the top of the ramp outside our two houses. It sat there alone, rocking slowly in the warm breeze on the edge of the narrow lane which passes between the houses.

When I came back, it was still there. Obviously, he'd left it to collect with the next batch of stuff, but part of me wondered if he had left it there for us to look at and possibly for us to use. I didn't, wouldn't, assume that as fact until, and if, he mentioned it.

Another hour passed before I left for my studio from across the village. After lunch at the local swimming pool cafe, I came home. The chair was gone.

My wife had left a load of groceries outside our front door for me to bring into the house. This is an honest village where you can leave things outside unattended without concern.

As I was bringing the stuff in, our neighbour and the man who was helping him arrived. After parking, they came to the corner where the chair had stood, only to discover it gone.

Our neighbour was not happy; he was in a state of shock. I saw him shrug a "where's the rocking chair gone?!" Then he looked down at me with my shopping bags and came down the ramp. Unlike his usual manner, his body-language appeared confrontational.

Face to face, he began asking me questions in Spanish rather excitedly. What was he saying? I was to find out later that what I thought he was saying was not what he was saying. I didn't even know what the word for chair is. It's *silla* in Spanish, "see-yah".

This is what I wrongly responded to, what I assumed he was saying:

"The chair's gone!" he said, speaking Spanish, as he rocked front to back while pointing up to where it had been.

"Ah, the rocking chair." I looked to where it had stood. "*Bonito,*" beautiful.

Then, hands on hips, I think he said, "Did you take it?" Which I took to mean, "Would you like it?"

I said, "Yes."

He became even more uptight. "It was for my shed," he said from behind his dark glasses. "You had no right to take it without asking me!"

I thought to myself; he seems very upset. Perhaps he would like me to offer him money. Kath's wanted a rocking chair for ages.

"For our terrace," I said, smiling. "Great."

The two men looked at each other and then back at me, nodding as though what they had assumed was indeed true! In unison, they both repeated the word "terrace."

Now, our neighbour's trying to learn English, but spoke not a word of it as he got more uptight. He was speaking fast and only in upset, furious Spanish. I couldn't follow but recognised he was not being his usual pleasant self.

"Can you say it in English?" He grimaced. Oh dear, I could feel him prickling with anger. Trouble is, when you get upset, all the years of learning another language count for nought. All your new Spanish words evaporate, and you revert to sign-language.

I proffered money, by slipping imaginary notes from my palm and smiling some more. It was a nice rocking chair, and I wouldn't have minded paying for it.

His reaction to this suggested the possibility of imminent violence. The penny had yet to drop for me. Most likely, he wouldn't have smacked me in the mouth; his mate might have done it for him. But he looked as though he was about to blow his lid. Luckily, help was at hand in the form of our lovely friend, Renata.

I got to our front door unbruised and shouted for her. Would she come and help? She's Czech, but her understanding and use of Spanish is miles superior to mine.

"Renata, can you translate? It's to do with a rocking chair that was outside."

"Yes, I saw it. Oh! It's gone."

"I think he's thinking we might like it, for our terrace. I would love it."

Our neighbour rattled off some words to Renata.

"Hmm, he wonders if you took it."

"Does he? No! Will you tell him it was outside an hour or so ago?"

Then my wife appeared on the scene. Now one thing I know about Spanish village life is that if there's a ruckus, the locals like nothing better than putting in their two dinero. So, I fully expected a small crowd to gather.

"He did not take it?" the neighbour asked.

"No," said Renata.

My wife clarified. "Someone stole it."

"Stolen!" said our neighbour, looking me sternly in the face.

"Must have been a tourist," said my missus in almost perfect Spanish.

"Whoever saw it thought someone left it there to take."

"It was for my *casita*," said our neighbour, shaking his head. Must have been a family heirloom.

And then the misunderstanding was over. Calm returned and the barbed wire was rolled up and put away. I must say, though, I felt a bit upset, thinking he'd thought I'd nicked his rocker. Guess I would have had the same suspicion if I'd been in his shoes.

So, we all agreed some rotten swine, not a local, had spotted it and pushed it in the back of his car and driven off with it. It's the tourist season. Stuff happens.

Later, I was relieved when I went down to our terrace gardens to see that it wasn't there! Guess I'll keep on with the Spanish lessons.

July 2017

The Menace of Melons

Summer's here, sultry, heavy, and hot. The little kids in the local junior school are getting sick with the temperatures reaching the high thirties and forty centigrade. Global warming is reaching its sweaty hand even up here in the mountains.

A perfect time then for something cool, fresh, and hydrating. How about big fat pink slices of cold, juicy drippy melon?

To be honest, the vendors of the manna from heaven who come in a van to the village to sell them, give me the creeps! Not them personally. I'm sure they are lovely people. It's the noise they make as they travel around the village.

(By the way, you will not believe this. As I write, the melon vendor has arrived in the village again. What an amazing coincidence!)

I'm not thinking of the fruit and vegetables chap who has a stall at the Thursday market. But the one who comes to the village in a big white van, with about fifteen tons of melons and two ladies selling them out of the back as it crawls along in accordance with a village regulation which doesn't allow them to stop. Well, they do stop, to sell a bag or two along the narrow lanes. The result is a bunch of ladies with carrier bags and shopping trollies on wheels trailing after them ready to buy. And a line of cars, frustrated tourists, and tractors behind them.

My wife joined the parade last week and came back with a huge load carried in two bags. She collapsed in the hall breathlessly. "Bargain, only five euros for four!" Unfortunately, it cost another forty euros to get her spine re-aligned the following day at the chiropractor.

I know I should have been out there to carry them, but I can't. I have a phobia about anything which sounds like it came from a military occupation. Attached to the van is a loudspeaker, a tinny old thing, and attached to it is a playback device in the cab. Therein lies the recorded audio problem.

I was born, like many of my friends, in 1950. I suppose, now, we're regarded as war babies. The Second World War was over by five years when I landed on planet Earth; but of course, it continued to affect lives. I can clearly recall my mum's ration card in her purse to be shown in the shops for her allocation of bacon, and the awful orange liquid we used to get poured down our skinny throats along with cod liver oil at the local family clinic.

Christmas stockings, throughout the fifties, at least in West Yorkshire where I come from, always had oranges in them, a special treat, as was an apple. There wasn't much fruit to be had in the West Riding of Yorkshire, or maybe it was in our house. I thought bananas were a rumour until I saw my first one when I was about nine.

Thinking about it, it would be difficult to get a melon in a stocking, although my aunty Mary *was* an enormous woman. Anyway, there weren't any melons back then.

Sixty-odd years later, here where we now live, there are mountains of them. Wonderful. So, back to that van.

I mention the war years because of the sound echoing around the streets and now in my head. I'd heard it in films and newsreels, a harsh, rasping, distorted bullying voice and now, to me, this sounded the same. Since all I could understand were two words spoken repeatedly, *melones*, (pronounced meh-lo-nes) and *cinco* (five). I imagined it was an aggressive and ordering voice, the repetitive message, louder and then softer, sometimes fading away completely as the van threaded through the labyrinth of streets.

I didn't experience the war years. But as a youngster I do remember being disturbed by black and white newsreels about the occupation of Europe when we went to our local town cinema. I watched fascinated as insistent voices in a foreign language made announcements through loudspeakers. There'd be soldiers in trucks with guns, touring towns and villages, screaming raucous commands at the residents in the streets. The melon van sounded exactly like that to me. You must think this poor old sod has had too much sangria, but no; I was thinking about starting a resistance movement!

"You will come out of your house into the street! You will line up in the square, you will bring money, you will buy melons, many melons! Disobeying is futile. You will buy, buy, buy!" And it repeats, all round the village. Well, my imagination hadn't worn itself out, as the announcement faded in again. This time I heard Daleks from the early Doctor Who series on the BBC. "Exterminate, Exterminate, you will obey! You will obey!"

I'm going nuts, I thought. This is vitamin C rich hydrating summer food not the end of the world. God, what would we do if they came round selling root vegetables? Cauliflowers have attitude don't they, never mind squash. They'll grab you and drag you down into the earth. I think it is in the voice.

A Spanish bloke who can't help shouting recorded the message, desperate to brainwash you into buying. Even Pascual howls. But then again, he prefers sausages.

"Awooo," goes Pascual. "You will buy my melons!" "Awoo," howls Pascual. "Four for five euros, do not resist or you will be exterminated, ex-ter-min-a-teeeed!"

I daren't go out of the house or my studio when the melon van comes round. I hide inside with Pascual in the hope they won't spot us and come park outside with the speaker blaring until I give up all resistance and buy a sack full from the two ladies in the back.

Pascual and I risk creeping out again when the man in the van with the scary fruit has gone off to intimidate some other village. Ours always appears deserted, as though someone has rounded up all the residents and securely corralled them in some vault hidden in a quarry on a nearby mountainside, under duress, eating great big fat pieces of melon.

Then we're out, in the sun-bleached street, not a soul, not a sound. And I see, meandering down the hill between the houses, a carefree kid with his pal, faces full of pink juicy dribbling melon and a smile as big behind it. And I know, me and Pascual are (again) just being, well, nuts.

August 2017

Prickle Scratch Sting

Whatever happened to the romantic campo? The campo of limitless colours and perfumes, of lushness and life bursting from the earth?

Come July and it's all gone to seed. The landscape gets mean, really mean. Though it's hot, you must think about wearing Kevlar trousers and armoured sandals if you dare venture out into the undergrowth.

It seems every living thing has pretty much given up the ghost and hates you for being alive. Plants want to prick, scratch and sting. Thorns appear on once green stalks. Where blossoms blossomed, nasty spikes appear intent, if touched, on getting into your sandals, between your defenceless toes, fixing themselves on to your clothes and coming home on the dog.

Even the trees hate us. There's an almond on one of my walks, weighed down with nuts in snug green velvet jackets. This tree seriously has it in for me. I dread getting tangled up in its sharp bony branches and having to fight my way out of its scratchy clutches. Standing by the side of the path, it bends down to grab you. Pushing your way through is like dancing with a barbed-wire bear. Why is it always in such a bad mood? And why does it want my hat?

At the moment, the campo might as well be in black and white. Instead of eyeball pleasers of every hue and combination, you have a slim choice of sepia cardboard brown, or dull mid-green. There are occasional flowers to be seen, but the other plants don't talk to them out of spite. They grow alone and forlorn.

What about fire? I walk slowly so as not to make sparks.

The risk of fire is ever present at this time of year. It's scary. And, as we witnessed in Portugal, natural events can cause fires, lightning being a prime culprit. In a recent local storm, a friend saw one start from a lightning hit on our local mountain. The *bomberos,* the Spanish firefighters, extinguished it before it got a hold—this time.

Even the ground itself is in a bad mood. Instead of nurturing, it has turned to spurning, hard as concrete and the same tone of beige. All it wants to share is dust and injuries. Stones, which in winter months lay there as they usually do, simply being stones, now want to roll under your feet and set you tumbling down the mountain.

Is it the sun that puts the campo in such a foul state? It burns down on plants and soil as though it's a deserved punishment. There's no shade when you *are* the shade. Imagine having to stand out all day with that laser light burning down.

Then there are the insects of summer.

Ouch, what a team of little buggers they are. Flies the size of toenails looking as if demons delivered them from hell. Mosquitos love human blood cocktails and leave annoying notes in the form of itch-burn lumps. My personal preferences are the carnivorous wasps. A load at an outside cafe the other day almost flew off with my wife and her cheese and salami *bocadillo* (a sandwich made with a baguette), which she would not let go of.

What about the "disco flies" as we call them? The ones that turn up in shady spots in their hundreds and chase each other around all day. What's that about? They ruin the view.

Then there are the geranium moths, miserable little sods. I hate them. You can't relax in your garden when they turn up. You have to try to catch them before they lay their eggs in your treasured plant and kill it.

Here come the ants, millions of them in combinations of sizes, climbing up your leg, in your bathroom, in the kitchen, all over the garden. In processions, on a mission, busy. But what for and why? My wife keeps our jar of local honey in a bowl of water after an attack by an army of them into the kitchen cupboard. Our friend Jan told us she does that because ants will not cross water.

Bees. Okay, you can't hate bees. But wasps are a different matter.

So, here's why the campo gets mean: retaliation! Spring comes along and boom goes nature in the most wonderful way. "Here I am," it says as it wakes up. "I was only sleeping. Whoo! What a fabulous world! Let's do our thing!"

That's great, but not so wonderful if you're a farmer. Because, though hopeless romantics like me soak up the beauty of wildflowers everywhere, farmers see weeds. Where artists see colour, farmers see a battlefield. Where poets find inspiration and lovers see confetti, farmers see competition and a fight for survival.

And so, to battle they go. It's a one-sided fight. Armed with weapons of mass-destruction for use on nature that won't bring a financial return. Pump that spray, boys, make it pay!

The first change of colour in the campo in the spring doesn't come with natural seasonal changes, the spraying of herbicides brings on the shift from green. And so, the campo goes from multi-cultures of naturally occurring plants to monoculture cash crops. That's why nature gets peeved. Romances can get ugly and by July, no one's speaking.

In a relatively remote mountain village that has worked hard to survive over centuries, there's no place in the physical reality of life here for the romantic. It's a hard life, and a contest with nature. Shame, but there it is.

When we first came here a few years ago, I thought the spraying in springtime of herbicides was terrible. I think I must have been living somewhere in a meadow in the *Sound of Music*, not in the reality of here.

The person who put me straight was our wonderful neighbour, José who is a farmer from a farming family.

He has a job on the coast, a very demanding one, and a wife down there too, and yet finds time to come up here to look after not only his elderly parents but also *two* farms, single-handed! The farms have been in his family for generations, now they are his responsibility. He's become a trusted friend, and someone from whom we learn.

One evening last winter we got into a conversation, difficult as it was in Spanglish. He talked about his farming life and the difficulties he faces working alone. We asked him about the use of herbicides and other chemicals on the campo. It was an awkward question to ask.

He told us about his two sons, of whom he is very proud. Both are at university training for their careers. They have no interest in the land or the future of the farms. In the past, they wouldn't have had much say in the matter. The land would have been their future. But today, young people leave the village and don't return. It's a problem in Spain today.

José explained there's so little money to be had working the land and the farming life is hard, in contrast to better opportunities off the mountain in the wider world.

"Me, I am crazy," he said. He'd just spent a couple of weeks planting more almond tree in the valley below where we live.

"Why did you plant more almond trees?" I asked respectfully.

"After me, there's no one to look after them, or the farm. Crazy, I know, but it's in my blood. I can't stop myself!"

"What about the spraying you do?"

"In the past, you would have family helping keep things on the right track, towards a good crop. Now I have boys in university and only myself to do the work that several hands would have done. Now that help comes in liquid form. I don't like it but have no other way. *Los químicos, the chemicals*, are my help."

I am so glad we asked that question. Understanding helps.

*Spring will come
and the flowers will open to the sun....*

July 2017

Pixie Painters

It's that time of year, early August, when heat and magic hang in the air. Our first Spanish summer in our new home, the month of fiestas and parties. It will be another new village experience for us.

On the first morning of the annual Summer *Fiesta*, when you step out onto the streets, you are met by the work of the Mountain Pixies. They've been here in the dead of night. If you had woken from a restless sleep, opened the window and looked outside into the dark you would have heard a rustling sound, soft, like rain falling on grass, or the flutter of wings, but not a whisper of a voice.

When we came back from the village square last evening, the narrow street between the houses was still grey, stained and worn. Now, in the morning light it's become a psychedelic trip to fairyland.

Leaving the house, you find yourself standing on a painting which stretches up and down the street. The village has had a nocturnal make-over. Pixie painters with fairy brushes and magic paint have made picture books of the streets, all of them. Each a different design, each a different story. A magical makeover, but not yet complete.

Then early in the morning of the next day, you wake early to fireworks going off. Between the booms and bangs there's another unusual sound outside, what is that?

On Calle Sant Antoni, where we have our little house, multi-coloured raindrops now fall, as overhead clouds of pastel droplets hang forming a tunnel of pure light shimmering in the morning air.

You have to go and explore. During the night you didn't hear a thing, like the first night, how did they manage all this? It must be a big help being able to fly.

Once again in the two days before the fiesta, you are blown away, the village had been transformed into Wonderland! Mouth and eyes wide open you leave the house, respectfully, bare-footed, as if you are the first to tiptoe upon a Monet.

It's still early, there's not another soul about, how *was* this done in one night? The whole street has now become a canvas, a 3D canvas. Paintings of every colour and hue appeared the first night; dream-like patterns, symbols, creatures of land, sea, and air, faces and lines that dance and coil. All as though a silent spell was cast whilst you slept. And last night the sky above the village has been transformed by thousands of hanging pieces of the fantasy dance, each piece part of a theme and all, by the looks of things, made by hand to one great design. It's all one thing, street, and sky above, alive singing with colour and dancing with the breeze.

Then you meet a pixie, splashes of paint on his tired face and clothes. He's one who has not made it home yet. Pablo, the tamer of the steel mule that I wrote about earlier, a house painter, and a talented artist. By the look of it this is one pixie who's been up all night. Now he's pale as the moon, beyond tiredness, going home to bed for a deep sleep and painted dreams.

Adéu i Bones Festes, Tàrbena! May the magic continue.

August 2017

Sleeping with Siesta

With all the troubles around the world knocking on the laptop screen every morning, I thought it a good idea to write about things of little or no consequence. *Siesta*, for example.

Since coming to live in Spain I've noticed that the need to have a nap in the afternoon creeps into your life, even when for most of it, it didn't; you stayed awake and functioning. So, I wonder, is *siesta* contagious?

You can't help yourself. After a few years, you behave more like the natives. Breakfast is between 10 and 11 am and so is the dog's. Your lunch slips to between two and three, or even four, and your evening meal amazes you when you look at the clock and it's getting on for nine. This is not especially problematic as a *pensionista* (pensioner), because you're not waking up at six thirty in the morning to prepare for the commute to work.

Escaping from the summer heat for a little while during the hottest hours, that makes sense for those who have grown up in a culture where it's an accepted part of daily life. It's so seductive, that lovely little nap, like the cosy bosom of your sleepy lover—just a few minutes, close down, lie down, delicious.

Trouble is, I can't resist a touch of guilt. Shouldn't I be up, not wasting the day, doing something? Every minute is precious, isn't it? How can you be asleep, old man? Ninety minutes later, the world has moved on but you haven't and, for the second time that day, you wake up.

There's another thing. In your sixties, it's hard waking up a second time in the day. It's like voluntarily going through your grandma's mangle a second time (you know, the clothes wringer on an old-fashioned washing machine). There's no adrenalin to make you lift your legs from the horizontal.

I'm not complaining really, we should be so lucky, right? Problem is, it's almost midnight and I'm full of beans. My eyelids are glued to my forehead, as awake as the rest of me, with nowhere to go but bed. With no disco, no wide-awake pals, only the regular distraction of several hours to come of rolling over under the duvet and fluffing up my pillow and visiting the tiled room yet again with the awful mirrors and scary reflections. "I'm dead, I am."

But why, I wonder, does it attract the non-Spanish too like us incomers? I don't see a rational explanation. Yet come two or three in the afternoon, we yawn and rub our eyes, as the need to take forty or eighty winks overcomes us. Many indulge in the habit, seeking the comfort of the sofa where they voluntarily choose self-induced unconsciousness, which in itself is amazing.

It's then mid-afternoon when the village falls silent as a grave. It's a kind of twilight zone when reality is altered. During siesta here you've no fear of criminal activity when there's no one about, because all the bad guys are snoring as well! Even my very active dog, Pascual, when I give in to a doze, does the same thing and falls fast asleep and wakes when I do. At least he's Spanish; it's in his blood.

Is it something in the air, in the weather? Could it be in the water? It could certainly be in the wine, beer, and food. Is it the culture that somehow and unavoidably seeps into you?

Yorkshire folks I know wouldn't dream of taking a regular afternoon nap. In Yorkshire we have a saying: "Time is brass." In other words, time is money. Here life is more relaxed under the sun. *Siesta* falls in the same Spanish file as *mañana, mañana*. Don't worry, there's always tomorrow.

I've never been a fan of sleeping. I know it's an inescapable fact of life. But as you age and realise you can never replace those days falling from the calendar, you want to make the very most of the time you have left. Spending a third of it unconscious during the night seems less than reasonable, never mind another chunk taken out during the afternoon.

So, I fight the need for a *siesta*. I'll do anything, tidy the workshop, fix that shelf, errands, do the washing up, take the dog out for another pee-walk, even, God forbid, supermarket shopping. Worse still, clothes shopping, anything!

It's useless. Whatever one does to avoid it, the urge is there to nap. There's something mysterious about living in Spain full-time which has seeped into you. It's best to give in and not fight it. Go and have a nice lie down. Close your eyes. Oh well, there you go. See you in a little while.

August 2017

Picasso At My Door

During the week, not having a regular schedule, I cross the village to my studio and once there, paint, chat with visitors, carve walking sticks or potter about.

If I'm going to paint, then light is the deciding factor of what time of day I go. You need the daylight to come from a slanting direction from behind, falling on the canvas from the left hand-side. Which most of the year here means the afternoon.

A couple of days ago I arrived at the studio and, to my surprise, saw some paintings stacked against the outside wall close to the door, and they weren't mine. This had never happened before. Who did they belong to? Are they any good? Were they a gift, or left for me to restore? A mystery on the doorstep.

There were five of them. All painted in oils on large sheets of heavy paper or card and old. There was no note or any sign of who'd left them there and no decipherable signature. It was a bit like finding an abandoned baby or your doorstep, but without the sudden need for nappies. Someone wanted me to take them in.

Four of them were amateurish daubings, no good at all. But the last one in the pile, though rough and unfinished, was a copy of a Picasso. Who, I wondered, would want to copy such a work by such a genius and why?

In the village is a German man who visits from his home in Thailand every year for a few early summer weeks. He is an avid art collector, and always comes to my studio, has a look round, teases me a bit and buys nothing. At least he's consistent.

He puts my ego in its place, because he knows what good stuff is and, honestly, mine's not that great.

Ok, artists like authors have to live with rejection. This charming chap, though, rather than buying any of my work, instead always tries to sell *me* something. He, I think, is rich. Me, I am not.

Last year, he tried to flog me a collection of frames, which he'd bought at a local village weekend market. I didn't want them, as they didn't fit any of my work and were ugly. But he's a charmer, and I gave in, and bought them for 35 euros. A year later, they're in my studio, in a stack, collecting dust precisely where I put them.

I wondered, staring at my unfinished Picasso, was it he who'd come across these paintings, and would he be coming round later not to collect thirty-five euros, but thirty-five million? But surely, he would have let me know it was he, and surely, he would not have risked leaving such a thing (if it was genuine) on the doorstep.

A day or two later, after having this thought, I saw him drive by. Was he leaving? If it had been him, it would make sense he would come to say goodbye and collect his thirty-five million.

I looked at the Picasso again. Pencil guidelines, quite confident in their execution, were unfilled with colour, and the brushwork was confident, but rather crude. As an artist myself, I know a bit about working up a painting from scratch. I recognised lines in pencil searching for the shape, not copying. This couldn't be the work of the original artist, could it? Don't be silly; a Picasso here in Tàrbena? Wouldn't that be something?

Scoff not though, things, precious things, turn up here. For example, the other week I was at the local tip. It's not a tip but an unofficial drop-off place for domestic rubbish like old mattresses, broken buckets, and lots of ancient worm-eaten furniture. I often go there; you never know what someone might have discarded, especially when an old house is being refurbished and they're emptying the attic and cellar.

Slap me with a wet, cold mountain kipper; the other week I saw this object, a bulbous thing. It caught my eye amongst a load of junk piled high waiting for the lorry to come and take it away with all the other rubbish. But this wasn't rubbish. I picked it up, took out my handkerchief, dusted it off and behold it was (is) the most wonderful thing. Three African portrait heads with a large carved leaf on top supported on the heads of all three, which are joined together. It's a flawless piece of wood carving and must have meant something. It's not purely a decorative piece of ethnic art, but an object that signified or celebrated something.

Carved from ebony, teak, or mahogany, it was beautiful and amazing. Now polished and in pride of place in our garden. I couldn't believe it. What a story it must hold within its frozen faces!

The village has a long connection with the French colonists of North Africa (that's for another story). I bet my best sandals that the African connection has something to do with it.

Stuff washes up in the oddest, out-of-the-way places.

So then, the unfinished Picasso in my studio—it's a copy, right?

August 2017

Summer's Children

So much of the population of Europe takes August as *their* month, special, almost another world, existing in its own time zone. Here in Spain, I think it's the hardest month to get through. It's draining. Summer visitors live life to the fullest during their stay, but some of us year-round immigrants wait for the fiesta bangs, bells, and booze to be over.

Today, the last day of August is the door which leads to the world of the coming year—September to September. The seasonal cycle is about to start over again.

Meanwhile, in the village, the transformation is underway. In a few days, the multinational resort that the village became for summer will dull the colour of its garlanded wings and return to its sleepy old self.

The houses are emptying of holiday residents. Cars winding down the mountain to the coastal highways heading for arterial coastal roads. Families linked by history and heritage say goodbye for another year; children are kissed, adults hugged. Next year, the kids will be taller and the elders shorter and some will never return. Shutters drop, doors are locked as summer homes return to their long silent sleep. Inside, the quiet dust falls, the old houses sigh, as outside summer's airborne visitors gather on the wires above the streets before the urge to follow the sun takes them on their wings.

If there's one part of the vacation that lasts to the last drop of summertime, it's the echoes hanging in the air around the streets, remembered in stone and eaves. Its sound is more memorable and lasts longer than fiesta clamour and party nights; it's the laughing collective voice of summer's children. Not just the current generation of village children, but kids from all over Europe who came and joined in their adventures.

Those kids of summer have had a wonderful time. Especially the little ones, the five-, six- and seven-year-olds who inhabit imagined worlds unbounded and untouched by adults and the often-awful news of life beyond.

I have lived in many places around the world, places where collective neurosis kept the children captive in homes or yards, where nervous adults watched over playgrounds. Nowadays, the addictive screens held in eager hands can also kidnap the kids.

Not so here. There are youngsters with smart-phones huddled in wi-fi corners. But there are fewer of them than village kids roaming free as children should. They look after themselves, yet they're watched over by the collective eyes of the community.

On a late afternoon, I was down by the cemetery taking Pascual for his constitutional. A boy and a girl screeched to a halt on their bikes. Excitedly and breathlessly, they asked me if I'd seen their friend. I hadn't. They were concerned the boy was somewhere on the rock, which towers above the cemetery enclosure, and that something might have happened to him.

Within a few moments, other adults appeared, as if summoned by some unheard call. I wondered, was a drama about to unfold? Then, another bike tyre skidded to a halt beside them. It was the "lost" boy. Problem solved. The little kids run free because, though they don't realise it, they're running about on the apron strings of the village.

A tribe of diminutive free-spirits arrived near our house in mid-August. Sadly, they're gone now. A small group of little girls and boys, different nationalities, locals, and visitors. They made their summer base next to our house in the shady cave beneath a níspero tree.

Over the last two weeks, high-pitched voices of excited chatter emanated all day long, till hunger took them home. They were busy fetching water from the *font*, stacking wood, building structures, digging holes, moving rocks, climbing trees and boughs, planning and building. Ceaseless work-play, urgently bubbling with purpose.

With amazing energy, the tribe filled their days in harmony, in imagined fantastic worlds as bright and new as their lives. Worlds which we oldies can barely grasp sight of from the leaf-litter of faded childhood memories.

Not once, day after long hot day, did we hear any of them cry, scream or argue. Busy as ants and animated as monkeys, with never a dull moment, their summer days in Tàrbena passed by in this way.

August 2017

A Simple Life

The lady from the hill outside the village walks every day with her shopping bag into the village to buy bread and groceries and chat the gossip with friends.

A man who works on the land walks to where he toils most days in the campo and checks his figs, saluting me as he passes. He was in the military.

The boy on the scooter speeding down the hill always says, "*Hola.*"

So does the elderly lady with the walking poles as she returns, head down, from her morning walk.

The men sit in the square every day unless it is raining.

The priest gives confirmation classes to giggling girls who think he is a Star.

The kids play football and skateboard on the playground beneath the school.

The lady in the *farmacia* always smiles.

A young lady comes there once a month to do your toenails.

The baker wakes at four and makes the bread.

The lady in the bread shop twists the paper wrapping your baguette so you can carry it home for your breakfast *tostada con tomate.*

Fran in the shop sings his song, just a few bars, when in a good mood, and his lady staff are always pleasant and wear interesting t-shirts.

People sit and talk, dogs bark, tractors are busy, the postman comes and smiles. The post office is open between 1:45 and 2pm.

The man on the big green tractor arrives to collect the bins.

It's Tuesday, the fish man and his wife come up from the coast.

It's Thursday, a few stalls set up beneath the church tower on the square.

Dried salted fish and olives, green plants, and underpants.

Some put out on display identical wares that were there over the weeks before.

Our neighbour rises early and goes to work on the mountain.

She places her stone from the pot beside her door so we know that she's not there.

The English lady takes her dog for a walk, one of many during the day.

Pepe, our farmer neighbour across from the studio, complains again about the weather with a shrug of his shoulders.

Later, he climbs down the hill beneath his house and returns with a bucketful of lemons.

The "ladies who walk and talk" come back to the village.

Toby, the little male terrier, sniffs about the village, hoping for new conquests.

The almonds are ripe.

The almond factory purrs.

The lady, aged 92, smiles and walks to the market.

The Doctor will see you.

The clock in the tower reminds of the hour, twice.

The man on the church steps watches it all.

Siesta comes. Everything stops, the birds hold still in the air, the clouds park in the sky, the olives stop in free-fall.

Another human day passes, like a stitch in a shawl.

Here, try as we might, we can't get the telly remotes to work.

September 2017

On Tour with The Duchess

1

There are a lot of British expats in Spain. Those who are not permanent residents like us are limited in how long they can stay in Spain, so they tend to keep one foot in Britain and one here, travelling back and forth several times a year. Our expat British friends who are resident travel back often as well, visiting family and keeping doctor and hospital appointments.

We moved to Spain to be close to my family. And Kath was becoming jealous of hearing our friends talking about their journeys back to the UK. She loved our visits to the north of England from New York City. It was time to make more of a visit to Britain and be like the rest of the non-natives around us, fitting in to the expat life of Europe.

Around this time someone told us about house swapping. That intrigued Kath enough that she went online to see if this was something we could do. After all, our house is comfortable and is in a historic and spectacular landscape with views of mountains that take your eyes all the way down from the coastal mountains to the blue Mediterranean. From here you can be on the Costa Blanca beaches in under an hour. Anyone would love to stay in it for a holiday. We would.

But after toying with the idea and looking around the internet, we decided we didn't feel comfortable doing an exchange with people we didn't know. So, we considered which of our English friends might be interested. It didn't take long for that list to shrink to the most likely candidate—our trusted, always good-for-a-laugh friend, Paul from Gateshead. He went for the idea immediately.

Shortly thereafter we found ourselves early one morning in the Northeast of England ensconced in someone else's house, and he in ours. We had arranged a swap with Paul who loves Spain, our village, our house, and us we hope. He even generously offered us the use of his old Hymer motorhome as part of the exchange. It's a venerable vehicle of *mucho* mileage that has crossed and recrossed the English Channel many times, en-route to Spain This was a huge and exciting bonus. We (more truthfully, *I*) were eager to try out the motor-homing life, especially as we had seen so many of them parked on the undeveloped beaches of the southeast coast near where we lived when we first arrived in Spain. It looked like an idyllic life, Gypsies, but without the horse.

On the morning we left, we dropped Pascual off for his own vacation at a rustic kennel nestled in a serene pine forest on the way to Alicante airport. As we arrived, he wagged his tail when greeted and fussed by the dedicated animal carers; he was going on holiday too.

In a few hours we had arrived in the Northeast of England. It was September and felt like whatever summer there had been had waned, and Autumn wanted its turn. September in the Northeast of Britain had been wet and Paul's sodden garden had not yet oozed from the cold northern dawn of hours before. We didn't hang about switching our lives about. We had come to know and like Paul over the last few years and enjoyed his company. Still swapping houses and lives is another thing. Would this, our first exchange, work out? We were about to find out, he took a taxi to Newcastle airport and there we were in trust of both his homes, one with foundations, the other with wheels.

It feels strange to be in the home of another, surrounded by personal things, his taste (he's a bachelor) and evidence of his habits. The house is lovely. We're fortunate to be able to use it and had visited several times as he had us. After living in Spain for a few years, we have come to think of it as our home in the UK.

To my American wife Kath, all things British are of interest. So, the first thing we did, using Paul's house as our base, was explore more of the Northeast, Yorkshire and Northumbria.

Paul had also given us the keys to his super-duper Renault sports car. Low, black, and high-tech, it was an unexpected bonus. Looking back though, I think we both should have had a medical to prove our fitness to get in it, never mind get out.

After a few days of the awful realisation that driving that car in a prone position, I really wasn't 30 something anymore, I looked forward more and more to exchanging his Gallic super-car for his bus-sized sofa of a motorhome. But by gum, the Renault did shift!

Ten days touring in his venerable motorhome was a hell of a contrast. The Duchess, as we called her, had a stately charm about her and wouldn't admit her age. Though old, she was reliable and for her size I found surprisingly driveable. Now feeling like pioneers, we set off on our final adventure before returning to Spain.

During the next week, our last, we dipped her tyres into Scotland, across to Galloway and up to Oban before looping back via Stirling and then back to Paul's home base.

The Duchess is something else. Our first motorhome experience was to be an education. I would love to see a secret video recording of us attempting to climb up onto the sleeping shelf above the cab. We're all belly, buttocks and flailing legs trying to pass each other in the narrow aisle. Only the English would apologise to their spouse for being in such a wrong place at the wrong time.

"Sorry, sorry," I said on our first meeting in the central aisle of the van.

"You'll have to go back."

"Well, where are you going?"

"To the front."

"I'm off to the back. The toilet. So why do you have precedence?"

"I'm the lady."

"Ah, right, sorry."

Same with sleeping on the shelf. We needed to descend from the shelf to get to the facilities at night. But first, on the shelf we had to get over the other person.

"Ow! Oh God, couldn't you go round the edge of me?"

"No, I need the shortest route. I need to go and quick!"
"You should be on the outside, then."
"Then you'd need to go, and you'd crawl over me!"
"It's dark."
"That's cause it's night."
Pause and sounds of loo door being shut.
Back at the ladder to bed, I whispered, "I'm back and coming up."
"Aaaargh!"
"What's wrong?" I asked as I pulled myself up from the last rung.
"That's my leg you're hanging onto."
"You've got another one, haven't you? Stop whining. It's the middle of the night!"

Yes, how nice to have a break and be in a comfortable mobile dwelling for a little while.

Our first adventure in the Duchess was visiting North Yorkshire, a rural area of great charm where I lived for fourteen years before crossing the pond to America.

Paul had disappeared to the beaches of the Costa Blanca and our little cottage while we were travelling south down the motorway in a behemoth on wheels, my first time behind the wheel. A baptism on a motorway, I was more than nervous. But once we'd got going and I'd got the feel of her, it was ok.

I soon realized when you're driving something as large and therefore visible as the Duchess, people take notice and give you space. It felt like riding on the back of a trundling elephant.

She wouldn't do much more than 50 mph, which would have been an irritation to other drivers if you'd been in a car. But an old girl like her, well, it's nice that she can still get out and about. On the drive down from Newcastle to York and then east to an area called The Vale of Pickering where we were to drop anchor for a couple of nights, I fell in love with the Duchess.

I loved driving her and soon lost all my trepidation. That first drive took three and a half hours. It was late afternoon by the time we arrived at the campsite in North Yorkshire close to where my second wife and I with our first son, Tom, moved to in 1984.

The weather, as we pulled onto the site, was dismal, "coming down stair-rods" was the apt North Yorkshire term for such rain. But at least this, our first campsite, was well laid out and we were heartily received when we announced ourselves to the office to check in.

Once on our stand, looking beyond the rain-washed windows, we saw we were surrounded by posh and expensive mobile homes. They looked as if they cost more than houses, with awnings larger than wedding tents.

I turned off the engine. "It looks as though we'll bring the tone of the place down."

The camp site was definitely up-market. The lawns were neatly clipped, the facilities were clean, and everything worked. There was even a place for washing dogs next to a recycling enclosure with a bin almost full of upscale empty wine and gin bottles. There were neat formal signs here and there, and toilets that you could perform lobotomies in. Even through the mists of rain we could see we were surrounded by expensive pieces of status symbols on wheels. We on the other hand resembled a broken-down old bin wagon held together by duct tape and string. Rain or no, we explored to get our bearings.

"Kath, let's dress up in our best rain gear, shall we?"

Kath waved her thumb. "And we'll use that posh looking umbrella of Paul's at the back."

"Honey, wear that yellow oilskin rainhat. They'll think you're the Duchess *from* the Duchess, an eccentric. Eccentric is acceptable in England."

"Why the hat?"

"Because no one but a member of the Landed Gentry would wear a hat like that."

"I'm American." As though I hadn't noticed.

"They'll love us even more.

"How about these boots?" Kath pulled wellington boots out from a wardrobe.

"They're a bit big but wear them anyway. They're called Hunters by the way."

So then we ventured forth. It was about five o'clock; hopefully the camp shop would still be open. More dark ominous clouds floated up and over the darkening moorland rim of the Vale.

The only people we encountered also braving the weather were a senior couple exercising their dog. They saw us come out of the Duchess, and almost choked on our affable "Good Evening." I thought the chap was about to be sick on the spot.

"I think they'll ask us to leave."

"Why?" Kath asked surprised.

"Because when the campers do their morning stroll to the immaculate ablutions, they'll fall over in shock when they see Paul's antique Hymer. Let's face it; she's ugly." Looking at the old girl when we got back from our sodden stroll. it was the first time we'd seen her in a different setting to Paul's yard. "She's looks like a motorised elderly Pug, graced with several window blinds held together with duct tape." I stopped next to the vehicle. "And we have a problem; we've not got the toilet tank connected properly." I'd noticed even in the rain, after we arrived on the scrubbed gravel and golf course lawn, she, being older and not being able to control herself with excitement, peed on it.

"Well done, John."

Luckily the gas cooker worked, and the shop had been open. Beans on toast had never tasted so good as outside the darkening monsoon turned into night.

Looking back from the darkening view as the camp lights came on, I turned to Kath across the table. We shared that smile which said, no matter, we're here together and everything is just great. All we had to do then, was find the bed.

Do you know campervan users wave at each other? Both occupants at the front, animated and genuine. Are you aware that doing such a thing makes you smile, then laugh? It does.

It doesn't work with people towing caravans. They just look straight ahead. Ambulance drivers and bus drivers, no chance. Lorry drivers—didn't try them.

Anyway, this weekend (it's now Sunday evening) I took my other son Adam and grandson Jack on the road for a dad and lads' outing. My wife stayed at my son's home in Foxholes, a village in the Yorkshire Wolds with our daughter-in-law, who was seven months pregnant.

The expedition went great. The six-year-old grandson acted as co-pilot up front (still on the platform of his child seat). He was Chief Waver for our vehicle and had a special hat for the job. He took his role seriously, hence waving at ambulances and buses.

Son sat in the back, strapped onto a bench seat, dreamily looking out the window at the passing countryside, chuffed to little mint-balls that someone else had the reins.

We wanted an adventure, but that's not what this is about. It's about Britishness; some would further qualify and say "Englishness."

I left Britain in 1997 for Provincetown, Massachusetts, USA, to design a travelling museum called *Quest for a Pirate*. The undersea explorer who hired me, Barry Clifford, is a shipwreck salvager and underwater archaeological adventurer. He found the remains of the Whydah, a pirate ship that sank in a storm off Cape Cod in 1717, containing four-and-a-half tons of stolen treasure. The job followed painful personal events in the UK, so I stayed abroad. Of course, I've been back to England many times over the intervening decades, but only for visits, living in the USA and then in Spain. I didn't realise over time how my Englishness, even my Yorkshireness, had faded.

Diane, back in Tàrbena, just had her 80th birthday. She's as English as the M25, but more cheerful. Di's a tonic on legs. On those legs, she walks her small dog Bugsy around the pueblo several times a day. I have not once seen her down, put-out, upset, angry, alarmed, paranoid, sad, or even slightly unhappy. She doesn't complain and is stoic, content with her little Spanish lot. As are the villagers who adore her. I asked Di before we left on this trip when was she last in the UK.

"Thirty years ago."

"Thirty years ago!?"

"Yes, never been back. Came here and stayed."

So, I wondered, is this cheerfulness *because* she's not returned to England? I mean, with all the miseries that seem to beset our homeland, how could anyone be happy? Or is it something in her British genes?

In our stately home on wheels this morning, the boys and I woke up on a slimy patch of concrete and grass.

All night long the rain had sluiced down on the campsite. Before we'd located ourselves in the muddy confusion of what appeared to be a post-apocalyptic scene the weather had turned from awful to bloody awful. Yet the holidaymakers packed the place for the weekend as if the lousy torrential deluge wasn't happening. They were stoically impervious.

It was getting later in the day, still pouring down with a stiff wind straight off the North Sea. Although the site looked rough behind its colourful banners and the area was a quagmire, I decided we'd stay. After all, it was only for a single night.

As the chap in the van next to ours put it as he helped us slither onto our spot, "We came for a chance of a weekend on a beach, but there isn't one. It's a cliff!" Note he made no mention it was pouring down, foggy and freezing.

That didn't bother the Brits. There were loads of them about in flip-flops and shorts, white as sheets in skinny tees and kids playing out as the skies emptied. Hypothermic caravanners were out and about, determined to enjoy themselves, sod the weather.

Everybody was merry. As I strolled about, those I saw embodied the idea of "happy campers." There were two men (this is 7:30 in the morning) chatting about caravans as they stood in the sludge. Kids were in damp sleep suits jumping about in the wet grass. Soggy owners walked soggier dogs as, overhead, battalions of murky cloud tankers brought more of the coldest, wettest rain.

Later in the day, after escaping the mudhole, the boys and I left to visit a fantastic place where bad weather would not interfere with our mission for adventure. It might even help it along.

The tiny village of Ravenscar perches on a dramatic high promontory of dark cliffs overlooking the bleak North Sea. It looms between Scarborough and Robin Hood's Bay at the highest point. On top, its gaunt and gothic hotel comes and goes as shadows in the mist.

We know this part of the Yorkshire coastline as The Dinosaur Coast. Its soft stone hides fossils in abundance, whilst the atmospheric setting has you thinking you might just meet one round the next rock. Overhead, you wonder, was that a gull or a pterodactyl? Whitby, just north of Robin Hood's Bay, is famous as the home of Dracula and as the port from which Captain Cook first set sail on his great voyages of discovery.

It was still raining, and the sky was threatening worse. But the boys wanted to go down to the shore (against my better judgement) and the downpour did not put them off at all.

We picked our way down the muddy path to the beach hundreds of feet below, where we expected to encounter seals, ammonites, and the occasional plesiosaurus. The rain came on heavier as we fumbled along. Thicker cloud and ghostly sails of mist wafted in from the sea. The kids loved it.

I was thinking, if it gets much worse, this track, such as it was, will turn into a torrent and we'll be stuck. By the time we were half-way down, we were soaked inside and out. My grandson had become a squeaky sponge, and my tall, handsome son looked as though he'd been in one of those contests where, for fun, people empty buckets of ice water over you.

Were they moaning, complaining, and whining, as the wind whipped, and the rain stung? No, not at all. I slithered down behind looking every bit the grandad with my walking stick, dripping flat cap and red nose.

We came across a youngish couple as they were coming up, with a sort of living mop on a lead which had once been a small dog.

"Morning!" the on-comers spluttered, laughing. "Lovely day!"

They passed on. Further down, we met two more people, a man in shorts with raw knees and oozing boots and a lady equally sodden. "Grand, isn't it?" he said, beaming. "Have fun!" she said smiling, "The seals are over there."

We reached the beach.

We scrambled for fossils and found the seals who, disturbed by our presence, lolloped across the slate grey rocks into the waves. But then, as though coming to the aid of their sanctuary, the rain and wind, with a low over-mantle of animated muscular cloud, got together and shooed us off. We were now in the teeth of an actual storm. A deluge was developing, and the cliff we had to climb to return was darker and more forbidding. It thundered, then another flash. It was as if the cliffs themselves were shouting at us.

"Come on Dad. We'd better leave." My son is usually cavalier about such dangers, but even he was getting nervous.

We made it back. Three quarters of an hour later, the kids were safe inside the gaunt, Gothic hotel high on its promontory looking down on Robin Hood's Bay and the dark cliffs. In the lobby where we planned to have lunch, it was warm and cheery. As we got there, I asked my lad, "Do you think they're going to let three muddy, water-logged wanna-be diners in?"

He nodded. "Sure Dad, look at them." I saw several people plodding up the drive. The rain had drenched them for all their outdoorsy gear, and they were gleeful, even though it was bucketing down, and the sky was full of thunder. They were still grinning and laughing through clouds of vapourised breath, and I thought, how come they are so happy? If this weather was happening in sunny Tàrbena, the locals would take it personally and no one would be smiling.

Half an hour later, we'd joined the wet, steaming walkers in the panelled dining room. Outside, the wind blew, the mist swirled, rain bucketed down, and lightning continued to flash. It was the best! No wonder this corner of England was the setting for Dracula.

Cosy inside and oblivious to the weather, over Yorkshire puddings and slices of beef swimming in gravy, the gleeful diners made the most of lunch and their company. The room bubbled with happiness. Stories of the storm they'd travelled through to get to their meat and two veg were all around. I overheard across the napkins:

"It was like a river!"

"Our drive is a torrent."

"I thought we'd be washed away."

"It's that global warming then? Pass the gravy, Alan."

"Could be the end of the world. Do you want those potatoes?"

"Never seen anything like it. Are you wanting the rest of your peas, Betty?"

"If the world is going to end, should we bother with dessert, Derek?"

As if to balance the panorama of the apocalypse outside the windows, as I was eating, pieces from the ceiling fell onto my plate. Based on personal experience, I can tell you Edwardian plaster is crunchy and may sink or float on soup, custard, and gravy depending on its density.

The English were being their most English stoic selves, getting on with it, making the most of the situation, and being joyful.

I'd forgotten that we're like that.

September 2017

No Rain in Spain

After three weeks of grey weather in the UK, we returned to our village to find very different conditions.

Watching the British forecast last week, a weather map widened to show Europe as a whole. It was surprising, as there were two contrasting marked areas that made you think you were looking at a map of two different worlds. The top half, including Britain, was cool blue, grey, and white with swirls coming in from the Atlantic. Whilst in sharp contrast, southern Europe was a solid blaze of virulent yellow and orange. We live in the yellow-orange bit.

This is the time of year when, normally, clouds float up from North Africa to drop massive rains on the land. Sometimes it comes as tremendous storms that can last for days, causing devastating floods. A storm like this is called a *Gota Fría*, meaning "cold drop."

So far, our fall of cold air has not turned up. The surrounding landscape, which turns green after the roasting of summer, did so for a short time after some light rains weeks ago. But it's drying out again, dying of thirst. Our second spring is nowhere to be seen.

This morning when I stepped out yawning onto the terrace, the cool dawn light was giving way to pink-gold and lilac over the local mountains, beyond which the sun was rising from the sea. I looked up as the last stars were twinkling out. The sky was naked.

The scene could not have contrasted more with the views last week in Northumbria. After three weeks of almost constant dull and damp, how wonderful to return to days under the Spanish sun. But I was thinking like a tourist, not like a resident with farmers for neighbours.

Down in the valley below our house, a tiny figure had long since begun his working day. He drifted in the murk of dawn, walking the stepped hillside amongst hundreds of his almond trees spraying weedkiller from a tank on his back. He has lots of land and cares for it alone.

It's Juan our neighbour. He is learning English and was glad to see us back home, especially Kathy with her being American as one of his sons is at an American University. When he comes out of his cavernous cellar, he steps right in front of our door. It's there we often meet.

Kath and I try our Spanish on him, as he does his English on us, becoming quite irritated if we attempt a conversation in our Spanglish, he so wants to speak English.

Our faltering attempts produce smiles and laughter because he's about as good as we are. Despite that, we always communicate.

The other day all were glad to see each other. After cordial greetings, his face turned serious.

"How was the weather?" he asked me.

"In Britain?"

"Yes."

"It rained."

"*Mucha lluvia?*" (a lot of rain).

"*Sí, mucho, todos los días.*"

"Speak English, please."

"Yes, three weeks of rain more or less," I said. "It's great to be back under the sun."

He placed his powerful weathered hand on my shoulder and looked Kath and me straight in our faces. He was serious suddenly. I've never seen him so sombre.

"No, not good under the sun! Too much, too much, no rain! We want English rain, is not bad, is good. It has not come." He shook his head. "Normally by now, but not come. We need much. Please go back to Britain and bring back rain. There's no rain in Spain." He went on his way, leaving us wiped clean of sunny smiles.

Later that evening, he passed along the lane on his tractor below our terraces down amongst his trees. I could see where he was from the rising clouds of dust billowing into a clear blue sky.

Later in the month a Gota Fria did turn up with all its attendant drama, fierce storms, katabatic winds thrashing the trees, dusty ramblas becoming white water rapids, huge and monumental weather. Gaia flexed her impressive muscles accompanied by symphonies of lightning and thunder echoing around the mountains. Yes, rain.

Rain!

Then it stopped, the sky turned blue, the stream beds and ramblas began to dry up. Within a few days even the memory of the great storm, which looked at its height as if it would never stop, had faded too.

One great big storm, or two, or three is not enough to fill the limestone sponge that provides water for the mountain folk and the town and cities below. It's not enough to assuage the thirst of the ongoing drought.

The locals say there's enough water in the mountain "tank" for three years. The catch is it takes three months of downpours to fill it.

Meanwhile the dun colours of desert replace the greens of life and the dust cloud above Juan's tractor follows him home across his land.

October 2017

Walk

Boots
Stick
Dog
Check the watch
Rings the clock
First step

Square
Men on chairs
Bon día
El tiempo bonito
But no rain
Again

San Miguel
Down the hill
Dog sniffs
Sprinkles walls
No, Pascual
He pulls

Past the spring
Running thin
Señor Pelut
Fills his jugs
Lifts them up
onto his van

Oranges green
Sausages
in lines
at Petito's place
Towel hangs
On the fence

Piscina wall
once fell down
Stands tall
Poor old dog
In the yard
Doesn't stir

Main road
Look left for bikes
On we go
Down the hill
Mountains high
Sea below

Walking
Morning
Each step
A word
A dialogue
Unheard

October 2017

Hammocked

Naps are good for you. Spain is all for napping I read somewhere. It's official. But napping can be dangerous.

I have different nap spots outside. Mainly comfy chairs in shady cool spots and benches with cushions. But the hammock is the best by far. There are certain times you can use it, and I don't mean the time of day but the season. Mosquitos love hammock season, or rather the slab of warm-blooded fresh meat that's unconscious lying in it. Yahoo! Lunch is up.

Just when you want to use it, in late spring and summer, when it's warm and lazy, that's when the little swine know that the hanging, swaying thing is an offering from humans to them.

However, even mosquitos don't put me off, it's so seductive. There she is, hanging in the shade, like a lover waiting to take you in her embrace. Oh, what a sweet embrace it is too. Once in, rocking side to side, just you and her, floating away in the air, it's just as luxurious and sensual an experience you can have without a license. And she works her spell every time, without fail. Within a couple of minutes, I'm off to hammock-land with my shapely darling.

Before you rush out and buy one, know they can be mean and treacherous. We hadn't had her long and to be fair it wasn't her fault. I'd got in eagerly without checking ropes, etc. and shortly after setting her off gently, the rope supporting her broke, as did my back, almost, when it hit the tiles beneath.

Dropping to the tiles courtesy of gravity and slovenliness is one thing. But there are far more unpleasant and embarrassing experiences that can happen to you when the napping and the afternoon dreaming is over: getting stuck in it.

It's so ridiculous that perhaps I should say it happened to someone else, some idiot who thought getting in and out of a hammock was easy. But unfortunately, that idiot was me.

We hadn't had it long. I found an ideal spot in a lovely shady place in the garden where cooling breezes would waft by. Having not attended special classes in hammocking, I'd not considered that there could possibly be a risk, other than breaking your back of course. With the usual dumbness of the man who knows it all, I decided to elevate her so she would be easier to get into, without bending down much, about hip height should do it, I thought. By being higher, she would rock further over a low table on one side and the succulent plants and cacti on the other.

The first time I tried her out at this new elevation I was alone at home with Pascual. My wife was on a mission somewhere and wouldn't return until late afternoon.

Pascual is used to me doing strange things and whatever I was doing with this hanging bag was par for the course. After sniffing it, he lay watching. I had learned after my first accident that the ropes had to be more than adequate for the job and secured with a proper knot. But what I hadn't done was consider the ergonomics of getting a somewhat overweight late sixties bloke with no head for heights in and out of it.

It wasn't too difficult to get in, not easy, but I thought well, I'll get used to that. Once in, she felt very different, tighter, higher. But I discovered that I had situated her where I couldn't reach the table where I'd put my phone and other stuff from my pockets. I hadn't been aboard for long when my phone dinged. I thought I'll let it ding. If it's important they'll ding again. It did, insistently. That seldom happened. My imagination switched into anxious mode: maybe it's Kath, maybe she has a problem, maybe she's had an accident, what if she's hurt, oh God. Or something more ordinary and the car's broken down and she's desperate to reach me. I had to disembark. I had to get to the phone.

How best to do that? I remember lying there and looking around, noting I was a good metre off the tiles. I know, I said to myself, I'll stay lying here and swing my left leg over the side. (The phone continued to ding, more urgently I imagined.)

Now, with my left leg swung over the side (and Pascual licking it), I'll try and sit up, hold onto either side. Yes, that's it. I sat up. Now, turn my body also to the left, leave right leg in hammock and then swing over. This was my plan.

I managed to get my left foot firmly planted on the floor, then leant the trunk of my body over, put the weight of it fully onto my left leg; prior to swinging over, my right leg helped with the momentum of the move. Swaying forward, I pushed down on the hammock. However, once the weight was out of the hammock, its more tightly secured ropes raised it higher than hip height. So, I had my left foot on the tiles, whilst the right leg was trapped in the hammock wrapped up in the canvas.

I had a problem. I couldn't raise my right leg high enough to escape the hammock. It was trapped, and so was the rest of me. One leg on terra firma, and the other at ninety-three degrees raised from my body, probably higher. The hammock had closed on it like a Venus fly trap, which didn't want to let go.

Luckily, and why I don't know, I didn't get cramp. In fact, I didn't get anything; the phone, a drink of water, advice from my dog, who just went to sleep. I didn't even want to pee. I did have my watch on, though it was no comfort, but I didn't have my small but very sharp penknife. It was over there with my phone, and coins and keys. I really wanted my knife, as after the first hour or so I was seriously considering hacking my right leg off with it. Though I knew it would make a mess on the tiles. And stains, oh dear.

It was a long afternoon. Kath came home just before five. I was still trapped, and the dog was now awake wanting his afternoon walk.

From the top of the steps down to the garden, she shouted, "Where are you and why didn't you answer my calls?" I called back a weak, "Help". "What's wrong? I'm coming. Are you down there and all right?"

I've never heard anyone laugh as hard or as long at another person's distress. The dog was barking, the wife was hysterical,

Sandra, our neighbour was shouting. I couldn't move. After a couple of minutes, they did help me out, and thankfully, when life returned to my leg and I could walk, I got the funny side of it too.

Later looking back, I had the pride of knowing that because of my experience, I had invented a new word, a sort of descriptive verb.

"Hammocked!"

October 2017

Laundry in Foreign Parts

Hanging out the laundry
beneath the Spanish sky
by the time you hang your shirt out
your socks and pants are dry

October 2017

Pressing Times

No apologies for writing narratives from a personal perspective. It's a traumatic time in our little village and I see my job as an observer and reporter. I hope you'll bear with me.

My wife and I have just returned from the council office. We posted an important letter (the post office is open for 15 minutes, from 1:45 to 2:00 pm), and afterwards signed a much more important petition to support the local farmers and wider community. There's a pressing reason. Let me tell you about Sunday, a memorable day.

Our day started as it often does by noting the weather; the gaze turns upwards. Seven a.m., sky cloudless, breeze low and from the northwest, sun rising above the mountains from the sea. It's going to be another gorgeous day in November.

Out with the dog. As a British immigrant here, the wonderful climate and glorious weather are easy to enjoy and appreciate. But for the locals, it's a continuing hell.

During our walk, Pascual and I met a local man who works the land. Everyone in the village has a nickname and his is Sordo. His name and its pronunciation are very close to the Spanish word for pig, *cerdo*. I always say it wrong, so I avoid calling him by name so as not to insult him. Our paths crossed; he'd been to see his trees and was on the way back to the village. Here I am in November, full of the joys of spring, but not so he.

"*Buenos Dias. Bonito!*" Good morning. Beautiful, isn't it? I looked up at the blue sky.

"*Bonito, sí.*" He carried on walking towards me, shaking his head. "*Seco, seco. No lluvia, no lluvia.*"

Dry, dry, no rain, no rain. It made me realise how separated from the locals we are in our experience of living here and how stupid to think that dry sunny weather, day after day, month after month, especially in the supposed season of the rains, can be anything but a torment to those who rely on it. Not a cloud in the sky might be heaven for Brits escaping the grey miseries of a British autumn, but a clear sky is a metaphorical dark cloud for farmers.

All week the forecast shows sun, sun, sun. There *are* clouds in the sky, huge metaphorical ones hanging over the village — the cloud of the ongoing drought and now the cloud of the tree-plague adding insult to injury. Here, where for a long while after arriving, we saw paradise, we now see it lives in the eye of the beholder, whilst reality is in the dust beneath the farmers' feet.

So, meeting that chap tempered our view of the weather.

But good news; at midday the fruit of the climate, the green liquid gold olive oil was going to flow.

Our neighbour Juan (his nickname is Rumbo) and his wife Encarni invited Kath and me to witness the pressing of their olives. We jumped at the chance.

Over the mountains in which our village is situated, lies an even more remote town than ours, surrounded by huge craggy mountains. With the intriguing name of Castell de Castells, it's only about 20 minutes away by car, but what a drive.

They instructed us to meet them at the Cooperative Olive Oil Press, founded in 1963 and through which oceans of local olive oil have flowed.

You can't rush the drive; it's all curves, drops, hairpins, and screaming death. We got there in one piece and straight away easily found the olive press. Several farmers hung about outside amidst crates and crates of shiny green, burgundy, and black olives.

Our neighbours sat at a table across the road, in the charming, shaded courtyard of a local hotel. We joined them. We, along with them, had to wait their turn. There are many olive growers whose crop needs pressing at this time of year, so you need to book a timeslot during the harvesting period. The Olive Cooperative building is quiet as a grave for most of the year, then it becomes crazy mayhem for a few weeks. Juan told us there can be two harvests depending on where you're situated. Our neighbour has another crop due in December.

He told us this year the crop had been a bumper one. I've noticed on my walks that the olive trees are heavy with green, red, and turning black olives. It seems contradictory; here we are in the throes of drought and these trees, growing in soil that looks as dry as snuff, produce all this fantastic bounty.

Juan's trailer sat just outside on the street opposite the co-op with plastic crates, stacked high, strapped down by cord and filled with olives, millions of them. Juan and Encarni wielding long canes had whacked each olive off the branches onto nets spread on the ground beneath.

After a lovely glass of local wine in dappled sunshine, his turn for the press arrived.

There wasn't much to it. There's an allotted time, which the operators attempt to keep to. But as it's Spain, with its rubber clocks, the appointed time had slipped.

Outside the pressing plant connected to the building, there's what looks like an adventure ride; conveyors, going up and down, water sprays, wheels whirring, leaves falling out of the air. Olives, in their raw form straight from the campo, arrive with leaves and bits of twigs attached, all of which have to be removed.

So first they're emptied into a subterranean hopper at a steady rate so as not to bung the thing up, and then off they go, up and round, just like an adventure-thrill-ride for olives.

Believe it or not, a powerful fan blows away the leaves and down they come, fluttering into a pile like green confetti.

Meanwhile, inside and out of sight, machines transform the olives from a solid to liquid form.

The de-leaved and de-branched olives travel from the outside to the inside of the building where an enormous machine squeezes them and extracts their oil.

We went inside to see where this was going on and were stunned by the horrendous noise. It's difficult enough to converse when you don't speak the same language, but even harder with fingers in your ears. Nevertheless, our hostess of the co-op did her best to explain. It wasn't a long or complicated explanation; the olives go in there, oil comes out here, travels to there and settles in a great big vat before being decanted for you to take home.

What you get is a thick and cloudy green liquid that needs time to settle, although you can use it straight way. This is it, the real and unadulterated green gold.

The growers pay for this service by the kilo. We didn't ask our neighbour how much, but his trailer parked in the yard outside was soon filling up with containers to take home. Since it would be a couple of hours for the oil to be ready, we said our goodbyes, thanked them for this enlightening visit, and set off back up the steep hill at the start of our drive back to our village.

On the way back to our car on the same street as the Olive Co-operative, there were several four-wheel-drive vehicles with boxed-in trailers behind. The wild-boar hunting season had begun, and these guys and their dogs had returned from a hunt. The trailers had solid cages with little windows through which we could see the hunting dogs, packed three and four to a cage, subdued, no doubt worn out by their experiences of the morning.

One vehicle had an open top flatbed trailer. In it lay a very dead *jabalí* (pronounced ha-ba-lee with emphasis on the "lee"), the Spanish word for wild boar. To be so close to a wild creature of such a reputation, even a dead one, is a memorable experience. For something so shadowy to suddenly take on such a vital form, even in death, can touch you deeply.

Part of me felt sympathy for the poor thing, whilst another, now tempered by our ongoing experience of living here, understood that from a human point of view why it and its greater family of brothers and sisters cannot co-exist unchecked with humans in this environment. For when it comes down to it, they are much better suited to exist in it than people. That's why they kill them. It's an ongoing battle.

The boar looked female, as it had no tusks. I estimated she'd be forty to fifty kilos in weight. There she was up close, so near we could touch her. Just a few hours ago, she was a live animal about as wild as a creature can be. Now she was deader than a doornail. Her bloody tongue hung out, blood matted in her thick brown brindle fur, and muddied feet. I imagined her hooves, the prints of which I see often throughout the campo on my walks, running for its life in abject terror with others of its clan from the guns and dogs. Recently she was out there, her long snout sniffing and digging, turning over the sod of the campo. There it was, now oozing blood through black nostrils. Her bloodied red and brown side was likely full of the shot that killed her.

As we walked back to our car, we were quiet, moved by what we had just seen. In the last hours, we'd witnessed Nature's green-gold liquid bounty pressed from countless olives and later evidence of the brutal death of one of her progeny. The beautiful landscape of untamed land side by side with human cultivation was all around us. It had taken on a vivid reality of life here in a delicate balance.

We drove home along the sunlit mountain road, not saying much. Kath looking out at the scenery, I drove.

Once back, we couldn't settle, so went to visit Sally, our English friend who runs a B and B in the village. As always, she opened the door with a broad smile on her face and invited us in. Lunch guests were lingering, even though it was going on seven. Lunches last a long time here, a Spanish custom of life the expat Brits have adopted.

By the log fire, we spoke with Tom, a renowned English painter and long-time resident.

I asked him for news about the tree-plague, Xylella Fastidiosa, that was decimating the local almond trees. The news wasn't good.

By order of Brussels, passed through to the regional government, official workers will cut down all infected trees and smash them to pulp as they stand, roots pulled up and burned. The government compensates the owners for their loss and fines those who refuse. Complete destruction of the trees was the only way to halt the spread of the disease. Our area had become a hot spot in the Alicante region and was receiving a lot of unwelcome attention.

We're only just finding out what this means in a wider context. All xylem sap-feeding insects are potential vectors. They spread Xylella by feeding on infected plants and hopping to other plants, and feed from there. The saliva of insects which bore into the trees transmits the bacteria, as they would do in their life cycle. Xylella gets into not only all kinds of fruit trees but also other plants.

Tom explained he has almonds on his land. The eradication orders he'd received along with others, call not just for the diseased trees to be destroyed, but for all cultivated plants as well within a radius of 100 meters, and no replanting for five years. Not only will he have to destroy his trees, but likely his entire garden as well.

Life and death on the campo. Our life in paradise was becoming grittily real. This day, in the face of death and plenty, was more like reality. It's a tough life here for people who depend on it and farm it, try and make an income from it.

The longer we've lived here, made our home in our elder years, the richer life has become as we saw beyond our initial dewy-eyed romantic ideas to a better and deeper understanding of what life requires. As a respectful observer over time, you gain more understanding, and your experience of living becomes more complete and rewarding.

November 2017

A Lesson in the Garden

Before coming to Spain, Kathy and I lived in New York City. We rented an apartment, and it made a comfortable home. But sadly, it had no garden.

The nearest greenness with trees, flowers and grass was a large cemetery, we could hardly go and dig a plot in there. What we did have was a place outside with access up a rickety ladder and onto the flat roof. From there we had fantastic views of just about the whole of Manhattan Island across the East River. But that too didn't make it as a garden.

When we decided to retire and make a new life, a priority was to live somewhere where there is Nature, and fresh air, and a garden, didn't have to be large we agreed.

When we found our place in this mountain village, it didn't have an existing garden, but we could see that it could, and within a couple of years, it had not one but several small gardens that came together to make one, and my wife realised her dream. It's still a novelty.

The other day I went down there (you have to reach it by steps) for a little private time. It's as quiet as it gets and peaceful amongst the shadows and the cacti, a good place for contemplation, meditation, and being in the company of plants. There are also the most stunning views of the local mountains, always different, always a reminder of the beautiful planet we live on.

Currently, residents of our village have become extremely anxious about possible environmental damage brought about by large-scale spraying of insecticide. The spraying is intended to kill the insects that inadvertently carry the deadly bacterium, Xylella Fastidiosa, to the almond trees. Almonds form one of the mainstay cash crops of the local agricultural economy. Without them, a secure future for the village must be in doubt. But the fear is that widespread spraying may do more harm than good.

So, there I was in the garden mulling over the dilemma of all this and though the sun shone brightly, the prospect of what could happen cast a dark shadow. Everything seemed on pause, at a pivotal place, the future of the village in the balance and all our lives along with it. At least here and now, there's a time for reflection and a moment of peace.

The surrounding garden was still, not a whisper of wind. Beyond the fence, the fruit trees, their branches loaded with blossom, were as strangely motionless as vases of blooms in a church. It was unreal to be so quiet and like a late wedding in autumn dressed for celebration. Further down the valley, almond trees, in naked ranks, bare, black, and brown, devoid of leaves, slept time away.

Across from our little garden the terraced hillside rises in stone-built steps, which are clad in squat, contorted trees, black of bough and trunk. They look to me like a parade of crazy dancing figures.

In the early months of the year, when seen in its broad canvas, the mountainside is an ever-changing tapestry of colour. But now in autumn, there are just a few splashes of colour here and there. The ravishing pinks of the almond trees dressed in blossom announcing the coming of early spring are now like old wedding photos faded to a sepia tinted dun. This is normal. It's that time of year. Nature is taking a well-earned rest. The wedding guests and bridesmaids have long since departed.

This apparent lifelessness prompted a depressing thought: What's all the fuss about the spraying? After all, the farmers themselves have already sprayed the life out of the campo with their own pesticides and herbicides. There's nothing left. Whatever else remains, they go out and shoot. It's all dead. Visitors and incoming residents can see the surrounding landscape in romantic terms. Where there's cultivation, whether it be trees or grapes or food crops, the farmers see it as an account balance. They have to.

I once asked our neighbour farmer why, when he is ecology conscious, he goes out and uses pesticides and herbicides on his property. His answer was as enlightening as it was surprising: he needs the help. In the past, it was traditional for the sons of a farming family to follow their father and help him with the farm and eventually take it over. That is not how it is today. I remembered our conversation earlier.

"My sons are away starting their careers in the cities. They don't want to be farmers here. Those days are gone. I'm the last generation who'll care for our land. The only help I can get, something I can deal with keeping the weeds and pests under control, is spraying."

It was a morbid thought, nature before us, dying of unnatural causes. I was about to stand and leave, trailing sadness up the steps, when a sudden small swift movement caught my eye. It was a mouse or a vole, too small for a fruit-rat. Dark coloured, it flitted over the rockery and disappeared. Stay still, I told myself, it might come back.

Then there was another movement; a line of green came down the limestone cliff that frames the garden. I sat motionless, only my eyes following, as, thin and sharp as a green pencil, it darted about on the warm rock hunting ants not yet hidden away for winter.

The lizard disappeared only to reappear a second later on the cushion of the bench where I sat. Perfect and beautiful, evolved for its purpose, the tiny dinosaur of the cracks and fissures was hunting for the next course of its endless meal. Down on the gravel again, it came very close to my foot. I wondered what I would do if it ran up my trouser leg. How long could I stand it? Would it tickle? Luckily, its sharp eyes spotted dessert and off it went again in a flash of green, so fast it left a green line on my brain.

I began to cheer up and stayed still hardly breathing.

Another movement, this time in the air, a tiny bird of no distinguished colour appeared amongst the jasmine foliage. It, too, was on the lookout for lunch. No larger than a hen's egg and with a hypodermic beak as sharp as a needle, it flitted from this to that in micro-seconds, before it, too, shot up like a feathered bullet and away into the branches of the mimosa tree.

All this action had sharpened my senses to what was going on all around me. I looked closer. The nispero trees across the fence weren't motionless as I had mistakenly thought; they were literally buzzing with life. Thousands of bees were busy in the branches and blossom, as single-minded as shoppers in a cut-price sale. What would we do without the bees?

Then something silver and mercurial cruised to my right; a dragonfly, as alien as any creature from science-fiction. To my surprise and delight, it alighted in a pool of sunshine on the table in front of me. Then took off, came back in an instant, wings all of a blur, only to take off and return yet again.

I bent down to get closer, pleased to be granted an up-close audience. Its four beautiful transparent wings and long red body, the twitch and swivel of its head; here was a creature as alive as my pulse. What an amazing being!

There were other airborne creatures, the little flies that seek the shade and appear to enjoy dancing. All day they hover around each other in circles, the disco flies. And even in November, they keep at it, as do the wasps, curious and pushy as ever.

I was feeling like Snow White, so I held out my hand for the dragonfly to land on, but no luck. It was aloof. Its little swivel-head surveyed the scene and me, then it too took off for the last time and disappeared. The memory of it will never fade.

Suddenly, nature wasn't so dead after all. Sir David Attenborough's voice came into my head:

"Here we are in this tiny garden in the arid mountains high above the Spanish coast, where only recently it was thought that wildlife existed no more, a place where Nature had given up the ghost, and retreated from the war. Not so. Stay still and watch!"

I raised my eyes as he'd instructed. In front of me, above the cap of the great pillar of rock soared two eagles, gliding in wheeling tandem on the current of air rising up the mountains from the coast, lords of the sky, looking down on us.

Where moments ago, I'd seen nothing, our little garden was full of life. Despite the monocultures, the unending drought, despite the farmers' battle to keep Nature in check, life in all its adaptable ways lives on all around, if we just take time to notice.

A Garden, the total life supporting space of it was something I hadn't really experienced and neither had Kath. Here we had a chance, if we just stilled ourselves and opened our eyes and senses, to see our little garden in its totality, an eco-system, changing throughout the year.

That's what it's become, more than what we thought made a garden. It's a fascinating world on many levels, connected to others and ready to share its wonders with us. When we slowed down and really observed rather than using, that's when we really "got" our garden.

November 2017

Up In Smoke

As I walked out one morning, the village streets smelled of home fires. I could see smoke rising from chimneys in the jumble of tiled roofs, a definite sign that winter has arrived early on the mountain.

The Spanish build their houses to be cool in summer and warm in winter. Most homes have fireplaces as firewood is plentiful for the farmers after tending to their trees and clearing their land. The residents light a fire in the morning and will burn wood throughout the day. I reach a higher vantage point, turn, and take in the village's panorama and surrounding hills. Plumes of greyish white smoke rise into the still air. The great burning of the trees has begun. But there's a greater fire, far greater than the ones that warm the houses.

I saw something that stopped me dead as I returned to the village. Out on the terraces was a friend, Stewart, a man who came here many years ago. He built his own house and vineyard, planted his own olive and almond trees, worked hard and long, maintaining the life he'd coaxed from arid land.

I always raise my eyes when walking along that section of the lane to see if he's working outside. I saw him one morning, and it's an image I shan't forget. He was making a bonfire of his trees, and not a pruning fire. His trees infected with the killer bacteria Xylella Fastidiosa have to be cut down and burned, by order of the regional government. If he doesn't, it will impose punitive fines. This is the major action affecting all who grow potentially infected trees. It's hard to admit, but its purpose, to contain the Ebola of the trees, makes drastic and awful sense.

I was going to shout up at him but didn't. I thought it better to leave him to his own thoughts, if his mind was anything but intentionally blank as he witnessed the flames consume his labours. As I watched from below, the flames leapt higher, and the smoke plumed upwards. The fumes signalled the end of a chapter in his life and a bigger closure in the history and life of the village.

The regional authorities had invited all affected farmers to a meeting the evening before. I expect they laid down the law hard. The disease is incurable and the only way to stop it spreading is to contain it and quickly.

The need for the growers to destroy their crops must be incredibly hard to take. Special inspectors identified five hundred sites in and around the village.

There will be fires everywhere over the next weeks and months. The growers will throw thousands of their cash-crop almonds into the flames. Smoke will rise over the mountain as future crops and income go up in flames, and the land will be empty of trees. And when the big storms come, as they will, the rains will wash the soil from the terraces and down the hill.

Other trees are at risk. If the olives become infected and must be destroyed, will the community remain viable? It's all up in the air now, like the smoke.

One can't help wondering if this is an example of nature's revenge. Has prolonged use of conditioning chemicals weakened the trees' own defences? Have sprays of this and that diminished their own natural immune systems? I have no idea, but you can't help wondering as you watch.

The hot and tranquil weather is perfect for wildfires. Fingers crossed.

November 2017

A Walk in the Words

1

A close shave today and I don't mean my face.

There are various kinds of walks around Tàrbena in the mountains high above the coast. More often than not, they are spectacular both in route and scenery. Pascual and I hike most days. Every time we're out we never tire of being in the campo, just as we never tire of coming home, late morning smelling my wife's glorious cooking, winter evening me having a brandy as he lies in front of the log fire after trolling about.

Walking every day, as we have now for years, you get to know the surrounding countryside like the back of your hand. When I say "local" I'm not talking about a stroll around the park. I mean rugged places, just over that hill, with wild boar, eagles, long-horn Iberian sheep and snakes.

There are many trails lacing out within a few kilometres' radius. You can change the combination every day if you wish. Mix and match. They originated as ways to the terraces that climb the mountain, the sides of which surround the hub. Over time, farmers and their beasts of burden wore the limestone rocks of the trail smooth. I pause, stand, and imagine the colossal amount of traffic of hooves and sandals it must have taken, aeons ago, to wear those stones down to be so round and polished.

Since we have lived here a few years now, I have not seen a single donkey or mule, but evidence of their former existence and importance is everywhere. On the outside of the houses, you can see rusty iron rings set into the walls that weren't for tethering your BMW to. And inside (I know this because we had the chance to tour the untouched and unrenovated interiors of several old places when we were looking for somewhere to buy), you will find an odd-tiled causeway beneath your feet, reaching from the wide front door back into the shadows where it disappears into a mouth-like opening. Indented tiles form an unusual pattern of squares. Why is this, you ask yourself? For grip of hooves and draining donkey pee!

The owners took the creatures in at dusk and (often, believe it or not, wearing what appear to be 1950s pointy women's bras to cover their eyes) down a ramp into the basement to spend the night in the company of other beasts on the home farm. But I digress.

Check the clock, eight thirty in the morning, time we should be off. No breakfast: we have that when we get back. Special K never tasted so good, but my dog prefers his own.

Outside the front door, I pause a moment to visualise the way we'll go. It's best when you have told someone (my wife) where we're going or leave a note. Even though you're within a short distance of the village and home, accidents can and will happen and out there in the campo with a sprained ankle, bleeding artery, or worse, you would be very alone.

Of course, walkers today carry their mobile phones. Sometimes, I forget mine or I have it but, oh dear, it's run out of charge again, or units or something. Or more usually, there's no signal.

I pack my kit in a green canvas sack worn on a strap over my shoulder. In it I keep essentials: half a toilet roll, dog-poo bags, dog treats in a small red pouch with a pull string, a purse, sometimes my wallet with my ID in it, and a screw-top bottle of water. Also, a set of keys with a whistle which I never use, as I prefer my fingers, when they're working, of course.

Sometimes, like today, I bring a compact folding fine-toothed saw, but I only bring that if I'm expecting to find suitable wood for my hobby, which is carving walking sticks.

I know I should schlep other important gear: maps, GPS gizmos, compasses, emergency blanket, tent, 300 metres of rope, a lighter, frying pan, a set of encyclopaedias, a Bear Grylls *Survival Guide for Life*, survival rations, machete, elephant gun, solar panels, and helicopter; but I don't. Just small light stuff, and a fridge for cold beer.

Yet there's more; in my pockets are my pocket-knife, handkerchiefs (large bandanna types can be useful in unexpected ways), a few coins that jingle when I walk, tube or packet of mints, and maybe a few more dog treats, which, of course, always end up in the washing-machine in a sort of Brown Windsor Soup with bubbles.

I wear strong walking shoes; there are rocks everywhere and spiky plants and you need good ankle support. Warmer times, lightweight, deep-pocketed trousers and, as the weather turns cooler, (a summer day in North Yorkshire would be cooler than here), hats of the woolly variety I have that resemble knitted patterned flowerpots on your head, flat cap, dark blue beret, or fake Russian with the flaps, not all at once of course.

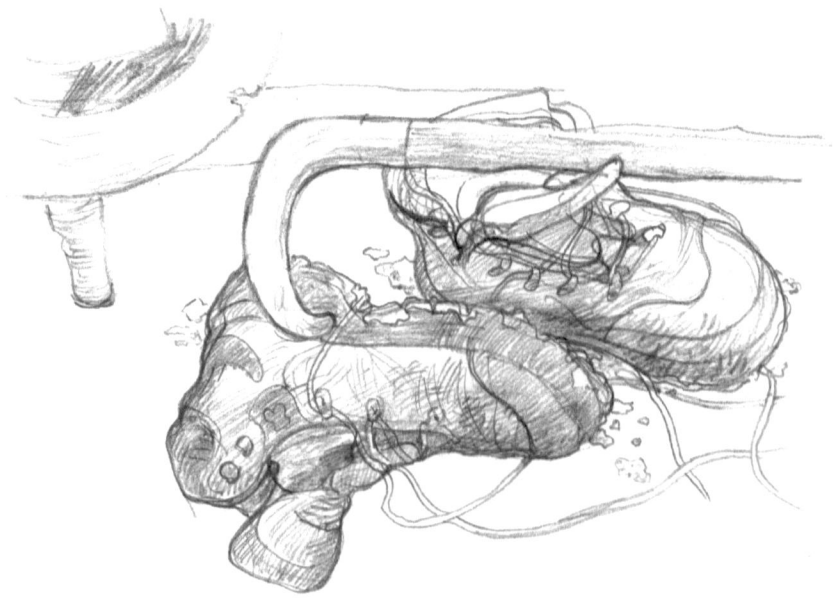

Pascual stays on the leash among the houses because, before we got him, he almost ate someone's little dog. But out of the centre, he runs free. I use one of those extendible leads that can be various lengths; it's made of a strong nylon band that might just save your life, or his, in a tricky situation.

We stood, the dog and I, on our doorstep and considered the route we'd take. Several days a week I do a straight there and back exercise walk, a simple but dramatic round the head of the valley walk, mountains to one side, Mediterranean to the other. It takes eighty minutes to do the circuit, six-point eight kilometres distance.

I looked down at Pas. "Let's do some exploring for a change." A message to the missus saying "out there exploring" might be a bit vague if she's trying to direct the search and rescue helicopter pilot. Of course, you can give the general area, but then you're likely to stray away from that. However, at least I can give a general direction, which is better than nothing.

The many ways out of the village involve hills. This is a community perched about eighteen hundred feet above the Mediterranean, that's five hundred and sixty metres and a bit, rising above the coastal plain. Though not on the scale of Austria or the Andes, it's rocky and surrounded by mountain peaks.

Every trail out of the place involves climbing up or picking your way down with care. That's why I have a walking stick with me, a wooden one, olive or almond made from local wood. They appear a little on the tall side. There's an excellent reason for that; you use it as a third leg of a tripod, to help you down the craggy path. A normal-sized walking cane would be too short for rough rock-strewn conditions.

I decided we'd go through the village, turn left by the almond processing plant and up the steep concreted lane. It leads you onto the ridge that soon becomes a dirt track.

The almond factory, the only large-scale business, is in operation during the harvests. This year, its prospects are in jeopardy because of this foul bacterium which is killing the almond trees in thousands. On this day, though, it was busy shelling those almonds like there was no future, which must be in doubt. The racket of the machinery combined with the hard almond shells passing through it reminds you of a stormy day at the seashore, when the waves produce that white-hiss sound of liquid energy as the pebbles roll back and forth.

The other deafening noise generated from the village (apart from fireworks and fiesta events) comes from the church clock. It rings twice on the hour. When you first come to live here you think, "They should get that fixed." But there's a good reason for it. When you're out where we're going now, you'll notice the clock peal, but may not catch how many bongs there were. You listen again forewarned as the second chime clangs two minutes later and this time you take in the full count. Of course, to get technical, it's already later, but being rural Spain, nobody cares about the odd minute here and there.

There's an old spring, a font emptying into a trough by the almond factory where farmers fill water drums. Several come in from the campo and load their vans and trailers with plastic containers. In earlier days, they would have poured spring water into pot jars and hung them on donkeys' backs. The women used to do their washing here in the days before electricity and washing machines.

I watch that font, the water emanates from the end of a pipe sticking from a concrete slab. It's a good litmus of how the aquifers are doing. In a drought, the spring, after a rainless while, runs thin and then dribbles away to dryness. There's something scary about a natural spring that turns dry. Fortunately, the other springs continue to spout crystal water.

Pascual licks my hand now. He's done all his major sniffs, and he's ready for a romp, so off and up we go.

Little did we know we weren't the only ones out there. Only, while we were starting our day, they were just going to bed.

2

The concrete track is steep and narrow. The farmers' tractors are compact, powerful, and agile, like the people. They are slender in design to manoeuvre the long thin strips of terraces, which follow the contours of landscape around the mountainsides. They make me think of Ordnance Survey Maps.

The word for terraces in this part of Spain is *bancales*. Like the pyramids these people knew what they were doing and built hundreds, if not thousands, of miles of them. I used to live on the North Yorkshire Moors, and there I would marvel at the dry-stone walls. These are the same, without mortar, the difference being that these walls, many over two meters high, hold backfilled earth and rocks of significant weight. The physical effort required to construct them in this most difficult terrain never fails to amaze me.

Many are hundreds of years old, dating back to the time of the Moors' occupation, which began early in the eighth century and lasted until the middle of the fifteenth. The Moors were clever people, inventive, practical, and resourceful. They recognised that by stepping the precipitous rock-strewn slopes they could increase the surface area of soil for cultivation, absorbing more rainfall, and by utilising the rock in the process, make the land more accessible and easier to cultivate.

On our track we pass the circular concrete water tank for the sizable volume of water to keep the pressure up for the village supply. Well, when there is any.

I'm not too sure of the hydromechanics, but like the springs used by the village, of which there are seven, our water comes from the surrounding limestone mountains. The limestone rocks of the coastal mountains were uplifted from the seabed and over time, water has worn honeycombs into it. When it rains, it drains down and they fill up like a bathroom sponge. The highest mountains in the region reach fifteen hundred metres. That's a lot of water.

In the summer of 2016, when many visitors came in the hottest time, the water supply dried up. When you don't have any, it sure makes you realise how important water is and how much we need it in our daily lives. For weeks on end, fetching water from the springs that were flowing dominated daily life—storing it, washing with it, cooking, and flushing the toilet.

I am of the belief that water, and its ownership will be the gold and the cause of wars of the future in a region that struggles for water. A little out-of-the-way place like this having its own springs will become very popular with the thirsty and those who want to get their hands on the liquid gold!

Water has never been far away from the collective mind of the village. The original settlement was higher up the mountain. It had water supply problems as the population increased, so they created a new settlement lower down where there were reliable springs and a plentiful supply most of the time.

The locals advise you about the springs once you have your feet under the table. You might assume that all the springs and the water that spill from them would be the same. Not so. They have unique characteristics, qualities, and names. One next to my studio is not to be drunk as it mixes natural underground water with waste run-off. Like the others, water emerges from a lead pipe and then pours into a stone trough, deep and worn around the edges by thousands of pots that must have stood on the edge waiting to be filled.

Through the summer months, the trough teems with mosquito larvae until the man from the council arrives in his official van and squirts something deadly into the trough.

The next closest *fuente* takes the form of an open-air laundry. It's only a few metres from the one I just described and it's across from my studio. For some curious reason, the water from this *fuente* *i*s not the same. It appears to have its own feed. The water runs out from the ground into two large parallel troughs. It's a beautiful sight; opal blue, crystal clean and available for washing out your rugs and everything else day or night.

When I sit outside my studio door carving or painting, I hear the water gurgling from the spring to my left and across from me in the laundry. I spend a little time watching and stay quiet. There are other users who flit in and out. There's a constant coming and going of small birds, especially in the dry summers, and cats they too come for a sip. Although the laundry does now have a roof over, it's open on three of its sides, enclosed by metal railings. An old lockable gate at the front creaks arthritically, but no one cares to oil it.

The water has a light mineral sapphire tint to it, inviting all year round. When the weather is hot, the kids splash and slosh about to cool off. No one minds, least of all me. It delights me to hear them screaming and shouting as I paint.

The water empties from the laundry into a big open tank where it's held for a while before coursing down the mountain. As with other springs, the water's passing through on its return to the ocean.

A neighbour to the laundry, and the man who looks after the key to the gate, is my friend Pepe. His productive smallholding below benefits from his share of the precious liquid. After a lifetime of working the land, he knows how to get the most out of every precious drop. Smiling and carrying a heavy bucket-load of that week's harvest up the ramp from his plot below the laundry, he's always a welcome caller to my studio. He often appears at the open garage doorway bearing gifts on his short way home, bringing up his pickings to his wife for use in the day's lunch.

We're both deaf as stuffed bunnies, but that never puts us off. He beckons to me for a bag of some sort, which he fills generously. In go lemons, courgettes, runner beans, oranges, marrows, whatever he's pulled out of his ever-rich soil that day. He shouts in my face.

"*Juan, amigo, mira, para tu mujer, para cocinar, para sopa, para comer!*" John, friend, look, for your wife, for cooking, for soup, to eat.

He kisses his thumb and forefinger with gusto. "*Sopa con crema, fantástico!*" Soup with cream, fantastic!

Happy and smiling large through his remaining teeth, he picks up his bucket and turns for home. I study the contents of the bag, so fresh; I don't get too close in case the courgettes jump out at me. Later, I carry the bag full of his treasure up Calle San Miguel across my shoulder on the end of my stick, like top prizes from a county fair.

Next morning, he'll be down there on his plot again, almost eighty and bent double, hoeing his familiar soil. His genius is the way he works the soil alone and manages the precious water.

He shapes the surface of the dirt with runnels for water based on the type of crop he plans to cultivate next, forming high edges to channel the precious *agua* to where he wants it. What he raises out of the ground, as if by magic, is testimony to his skill as a grower and his knowledge accrued over decades of working with the land, the sun and, most importantly, what springs out of the mountain.

As you pay close attention to the locals, you realise there's so much to learn.

3

The wild animals that live in the campo are constantly in search of food and water. As we continue our walk the dogs on our left barked their heads off with big barks, little whiny squeals and several sounds in between. There are many dogs in the village, but few pets. Galgos and Podencos, working dogs, are common and are the most popular breeds for hunting.

As a dog-lover, I found the way the locals treat these dogs hard to take sometimes. They usually confine them in dog-runs and keep them hungry as it makes them sharper and keener when released on the hunt. The animals are commodities and kept for one purpose—hunting.

Come hunt day, the dogs are loaded in a trailer and transported early to the chosen location. When you pass such a trailer, you see lots of dog faces, animated and barking, crammed together inside.

This is a sure sign the affair will soon begin. I can only imagine what it must be like on a hunt. I see the results when the hunters bring the dead boar back to the village, laid out on the ground close to a roadside bar. Medical personnel are removing the offal and taking samples, obviously a legal requirement. I stand and stare; Pascual doesn't even sniff in their direction. For things alive only a little time ago, they lie prostrate, sometimes bloody, and awfully dead.

I have no sentimental affections for the wild boar. They are a menace, a living destructive force, which threatens to overwhelm the land-based community in places like these. I would have warmer feelings for them if I lived in a town. But living here for a while and walking in the landscape that they and men frequent, I can see the damage they do. They need to be kept in check. In the past, a workforce from the village would repair the broken walls and damage to crops. But now there are few younger people staying on in farming. The farmers who are here are well aware they are likely to be the last of their line. So, the collapsed walls lie where they fall. It often looks like the aftermath of a battle, hard to believe that a family of medium-sized creatures could do such damage.

The only recourse the farmers have is to hunt them in order to cull their numbers. There's also an arrangement for hunters from outside to come on organised culls. In the autumn months the council office tapes information posters to the walls. I always look for those posts. Even in Spanish, I can understand where not to go that weekend. The most likely time to encounter them is on a walk, especially early in the morning or at dusk, and much more likely if you're out at night. They've changed their natural routine to be nocturnal animals, foraging at night to avoid the guns and dogs.

We are walking now in an area where we once came near to a family of them. Today, Pascual went on alert in front of me on the track, hidden by foliage, about 20 meters away. What it must be like to have the senses of a cat or a dog. I can't hear or smell a thing! They could be playing trombones and eating mustard hot-dogs for all I knew. To him, they were close, and he knew where and what they were.

He began to bark. It was different; not a rising, excited, aggressive bark as he would make if he saw a wild goat; rather a halted, restrained, controlled bark-pause-bark. He was communicating.

As I rounded the bush, I came to a halt and grasped my heavy stick tighter, for he was on full alert; stock-still, limbs like table legs, hackles up, tail up and bent over his back, ears at full stretch. The boar were below us in the undergrowth, settling down for a nice day's nap in the grassy undergrowth.

With other wild animals like wild goats, he would be off by now, running at full pelt towards them. But he had no intention of mixing it with these denizens of the campo. He's a smart dog and

I expect, because of previous encounters, he knows when to avoid danger and unnecessary injury. Wild boar, especially if they think their small ones are in danger, will defend themselves and attack fearlessly and aggressively. A boar injured a villager only last year.

I looked down at the area where he had fixed his eyes. I saw the brush move as several brown squat bodies in a short line sidled away from under the vegetation. He stopped barking. We stood both still as one and watched them saunter, unconcerned, disappearing into deeper vegetation.

There were several more almost encounters, often as though you had arrived on a scene where they were just moments ago. One such time, I was out on an ordinary morning walk close to the village and on a familiar trail. This particular morning, the little voice, which gets me into trouble sometimes, said, we didn't see that track before, did we? Come on old man—let's follow it!

I could see the boar had used it recently. Besides the footprints in the muddy path, there were many holes on either side with damp soil thrown up where they'd been grubbing for roots. The track disappeared under the dense foliage of mountain olive trees. As I was bending down to avoid low branches, I didn't realise where it was leading. Pascual was in front, but not far ahead.

The bushes lifted higher, and we were in a kind of green cave, with a clearing below, rather like an arbour. It was a beautiful space, sort of magical and only a few hundred metres down the valley from village buildings.

I looked around, as did Pascual, sampling the air as he did so. There were no other creatures there, only him and me. My eyes adjusted to the twilight beneath the foliage above and I realised where we were. It was the equivalent of a Turkish bath house, for there in front of us, surrounded by several freshwater pools, was a still-steaming mud-wallow; a shallow depression filled with mud and brown smelly water. I almost expected a boar to appear from the bushes with a big sponge and branch to smack. Though there were no towels hung on the branches, this place showed all the signs that it had recently been in use, minutes or even seconds before.

There were lots of hoof prints, some just filling with water. It felt like we had wandered into the bad guys' hidden lair. And any moment, bad mad Boar Bruno would appear out of the steam and shadows in a towel carrying a Tommy gun levelled at us.

Needless to say, we haven't been there since.

Walking the same route home, the dogs in the pen recognised we were only passing by and acknowledged our presence with whines and whimpers. Rising higher out of the village, the track turns from concrete to dirt and broken bricks, tiles, and stones beneath your feet. Meanwhile the vista opens up to almond and olive trees groves, stretching and curving away on broad terraces.

The almond season was coming to its close. Workers were out amongst the trees with their long canes, knocking the last of the nuts onto nets spread wide around their trunks. It may look picturesque in a pre-industrial way, but by gum, it must be tough hard work—arduous, dirty, and tedious. One consequence of rattling a tree like this is what lands in your hair if you forgot your hat; a menagerie of little creatures, so I have been told, some pleased by your choice of shampoo and conditioner, others keen on making a new home in your ear.

Oblivious to such concerns, amongst the almond trees, was a neighbour of ours waving a cane in the branches. She works alongside her farmer employer. She has with her a big scary dog, a German Shepherd, which is always on guard. She's protective of her human pack, and, as expected, began barking ferociously. Pascual and she were puppies at the same time in the village and although barking when they meet, there's been no real bother.

Pascual was off the lead, and out of sight. I whistled for him. Out of the trees he bounded, eyes bright, tongue hanging pink, running back towards me. Then he turned and ran further on up the path where the little mountaintop flattens and disappears. He knows we're heading home.

On either side, the mountains rise like scenery on the grand and gob-smacking stage of nature. It's a sensual treat that speaks to all your senses, always changing, always alive. Ninety-nine percent of the time, nothing bad happens. But there's always a chance of that one percent. The close shave today could have been that one percent. No two walks are the same.

November 2017

Another Terrible Beautiful Day

Late in the year, darkness is thickening earlier as heavy cloud rolls over the mountains. Pascual, who's been napping close to my workbench in the studio stands up, looks at me. He's not on a lead and goes to the open outside door. After a look and a sniff, he turns back to me. The streetlights came on as he did that.

"Ok, is it time for home?" He wagged his tail. He knows the word home and all that it means.

I set down the walking stick I was carving, gave it one last look for the day and then a cursory tidy up of tools.

Outside, with a huge bang, the garage door rolled down to the concrete below. I looked up at the mountains. They'd disappeared in a thick veil of cloud; a sure sign rain was imminent.

"Come on before we get soaked."

Pascual caught a sense of it as he scurried, pulling me along with dog-urgency (he hates getting wet) and up the hill between the closed-up houses, along Calle San Miguel, now brightly lit, to the empty square. I glanced into the interior of the bar, empty, with expectant stools at the bar. It looked like a Hopper painting. Then the short distance to home. The first rain drops fell. Pascual kept touching and licking my hand as we walked as if to say, come on old man.

We headed down San Antonio, our bottle-necked, narrow street, and down the ramp to the front of our house. Open the gate, key in the front door lock, Pascual's tail wagging faster. Fat raindrops splashed around us. Standing there, under the shelter of the glass awning, Pascual was relieved.

Our neighbour popped out of her door with a great big toothy smile on her face, stuck up her thumb and punched the sky with it. "Rain, *lluvia*, yeah!"

We were inside, warmth and sweet smells wrapped us up like a beach towel on a cold day. I stood and looked at our lovely little place, all the home we need now.

Kath ran down the stairs. "There's a *big* storm coming our way. Big hailstones. Katherine texted. It's happening in Jalon now, teeming down they're saying. Pouring, and stones this size!" She showed a one-inch gap between her fingers.

Here, when it rains, you want to dance and sing. It's the same feeling I remember when we were little kids, as the first snowflakes fell on the dark brick yard. Only here we'll take plain *agua*, thanks. No need for novelty.

The drought is turning this place to dust. In the autumn, wet weather should begin. It's arrived on time for centuries apparently. The agricultural season depends on it, a key moment in the natural cycle of things, replenishment. But now, new weather patterns have broken the cycle.

The rains haven't turned up, apart from a shower here and there. This is the season, after summer, when the rains should have arrived like a welcome cloud-borne tsunami and turned the land green with fresh growth, the second spring. It's not green; everywhere it's the colour of cardboard. We have only been here a few years, but we share in the locals' deep disappointment.

What was happening outside was a big deal, but would it be short-lived? Every drop counts. I opened the door It was pouring and looked as though it was setting in for the day, the week maybe. How about a month?

"Do you fancy a walk?" I asked.

"What?

"Come on, we might not see it again.'

"What?"

"Rain."

"You'll dissolve, your skin is not used to water John; you'll be washed away."

"I'm not going to get wet. I'm going to wear my new waterproof cape with the hood."

"See you."

"Are we having something waterproof to eat for a telly dinner?"

"Fish fingers," she shouted as I opened the door. Pascual was looking at me.

"You want to come?" Smart dog: he went and hid under the wormwood table.

It was like stepping out into a waterfall. I was dry inside my cape, the first time I'd used it. I was relieved it wasn't stormily windy; a mountain blusty-gust I am sure could pick me up and deliver me in another country, and I hadn't brought my passport!

The village clings to the top of a mountain, lumpy and bumpy. The only level place is the village square in front of the church.

Everywhere else is tilted, which rain just loves, as the real reason it's falling to earth is to make its way back to its home, the ocean, pronto. A white-water rapid had formed as it flowed joyously just outside the front door down the steep track to the gorge below our houses.

The village had acquired new streetlights, very bright ones. The light illuminating the rain was magical, the sound of the rain was part of that magic. I'd risked keeping my hearing aids in and hoped they would stay dry under the waterproof hood. The hood amplified the sounds, the village hissed with a billion, raindrops falling to the street, the roofs, the steps, washing the remains of the summer heat away, a back scrub, a front scrub, an all-over scrub.

I walked along San Antonio, the houses on both sides with shutters drawn as though to shut out what it was they craved. The doorways are fitted with wooden panels to stop the rain from seeping through the front doors. The streets, the alleyways as the deluge continued, became rivers, fantastic living water blessing the old place.

I stepped into the square, with its one bright door, the open bar, where a small group of locals had gathered at the front door obviously happy to see the rain fall. They were celebrating, drinks, cigarettes, and laughter framed by the light behind them as it poured down. It could have been raining champagne.

November 2017

Morning Bell

Dawning
in the village
to the sound of the bell
a soul passed

while we were sleeping
who, we cannot tell

Was it a man
woman, child
aged
gracious, or hated
loved, reviled, loud,
understated
who, we don't know

Was it him in the hat
or the lady with cats
the child that cried
was it a baby that died
or was it someone
whose work was not yet done

The church doors are open
the time has come
wake up
be grateful
for whom
the bell rung

October 2017

Of Dogs and Saints and Cemeteries

There are numerous national holidays in Spain, many of which are of religious origin. One of the most important is All Saints' Day.

On previous evenings, the spectres of waifs haunted the village in bedsheets, wispy dresses, torn blood-stained clothes and faces which looked as though they shaved themselves with a chainsaw. No, not the locals; their kiddies.

In and out of the lanes they danced and screamed, as un-scary as a toy shop with a sale on. Kath bought a sack full of sweets (candy she calls it, she can't help it, she's American) fully expecting ghouls to be turning up by the school-load for treats.

But no, not one knock or maniacal laugh at the door. It could be our dog, Pascual, and his reputation for being an effective guard dog that put the little devils off. Anyway, we've now got all this candy. I expect it will be with us until next Halloween.

We live on an odd little corner, with two neighbours, both Dutch and both lovely. The lady opposite, who is in her eighties (though you wouldn't think so), has a thing about witches. She has a van in which she tours Europe in the summer months. An unexpected collection of little witch figures covers the dashboard. Some people have hanging furry dice; she has witches. Well, the local children have noticed, and I think some of them now think that she is one.

Last year at Halloween, she discovered her house had been the target of an egg attack. She opened her door after hearing noises outside to find yolk running down her walls and windows. Also last year, our direct neighbour, a younger woman, had rocks thrown at her house. A bunch of little girls were the culprits. So far, our home has escaped their interest. This year surprisingly has been peaceful.

The day before All Saints' Day there was a very special quietness about the village, a reverent atmosphere. From our kitchen terrace we can see the cemetery across the valley, where there was a lot going on. People were quietly coming and going.

On one morning walk, as Pascual and I strode purposefully through the village, we came across several locals, all of whom we know, at least by sight, carrying beautiful flower arrangements. These were the busy ones we'd seen on their way to dress the graves of their dearly departed.

The village cemetery floats like an anchored ship tethered in the sky. White walls enclose a rectangular enclosure. Behind it a mountain top rises sheer and craggy and further behind, other higher peaks, and beyond them, the blue of the sea. When a cloud comes in and up, it becomes a cruise-liner for the spiritual remains of generations still connected to the village, tethered by the lane which runs up a steep hill and passes the school at the top before becoming entangled in the jumble of houses occupied by the living.

Halloween morning, I watched some of the living making their way down there. They looked from our vantage point like ants carrying floral tributes, which they'd gathered in the campo. When they got there, they disappeared through the tall arched gate into the ship of souls and out of sight.

All Hallows E'en is the day when, to prepare for the Saints' arrival, family members dress the graves in flowers. We went down there late in the afternoon to take a peek and also to place a photograph on the grave of Salvador, a man we didn't know but to whom we owe a lot. He was living history, for he was the last shepherd of the village.

The cemetery is a delightful and peaceful place, cared for by local ladies. Unlike English church graveyards with coffins buried in the ground, here the incumbents occupy niches in the walls.

The Spanish inter their deceased quickly, within 24 to 48 hours. Funerals in the village are quite dramatic events. The bells toll the funeral knell, so everyone knows someone has died. There's a service at the church in the square. Afterwards the mourners follow the hearse, slowly walking out of the village. They pass the carpenter's workshop, the bakery, the school then silently down the lane leading to the final resting place, the ship of souls. There, helpers insert the coffin into the open tomb in the wall and immediately brick it up.

After having placed a photograph of Salvador and Pascualet by his tombstone the day before on Halloween, we walked down in the thickening twilight to reclaim the photo which his former lady friend in the village had given us.

Even though the cemetery was almost in the dark by the time we got there, light spilled in from the streetlamps outside, enough to see. All Saints' Day had come and gone and yet even in the gloom the place sparkled and glowed with life and the colours of a thousand flowers arranged on hundreds of graves. In the thickening mountain twilight, we walked through the parade of yew trees turning right to Salvador's tomb.

I always expected Pascualet, who was at our side, to howl or bark or do something as we approach his former owner's grave. But he didn't react. I wondered if he would recognise Salvador from the photo on the marble tablet of him and his brother, with whom he was now incarcerated. But no, he was quiet and sat there without being told.

On the shelf where we had left it, stood the photograph of Salvador with Pascual standing on the corner, but now Pascual was here at my side standing by his grave.

As we took a moment to take in the atmosphere, in the shadows, a figure moved. It was the lady in the dressing gown from the village. She was going from one grave to another, touching and caressing the petals of the flowers. She didn't speak as we left and Pascualet made no sound.

We walked quietly and thoughtfully home up the hill to the village, Pascual between us.

November 2017

Rubbish

I suppose we take rubbish for granted; I mean, its removal. You bag it or stack it and take it and leave it and it goes away, carefully sorted for recycling. Even on top of a mountain, it's the same. A truck lumbers up the road from the coast with its tortuous bends and when arriving at the village, men in green uniforms and high-viz stripes on their trousers pull levers at the back and in it goes, disappeared, gone. Where? I have no idea.

Sometimes there's a long period between collections, especially of the larger bulkier stuff, the stuff that my dreams are made of.

Decades ago, I worked in England in the beautiful city of York. York was a fascinating place to be because you were literally living on top of its history. I learned something about rubbish while working on the Jorvik Viking Centre.

There are two sides to archaeology. One is about the material that doesn't decompose. The other part is organic. Humans dump stuff, which is forgotten, discarded, dropped left to rot, and ages later, rediscovered. Ordinary day-to-day waste from a thousand years ago, as precious as any silver hoard. Because a thousand-year-old preserved leather shoe can take you on a factually based journey back in time.

So it was with the archaeological site deep below the streets of York. There, the archaeologists dug down about four metres, where in the wet conditions detritus of another age lay preserved. The blueprint in hard material and organic form was to provide comprehensive data for the most ambitious reconstruction of life lived in a far-off time.

Working on that extraordinary project and having contact with professional archaeologists changed the way I looked at places. I came to understand how human waste, what we throw away in one form or another, was the foundation of human history. I became fascinated by it. Our rubbish is evidence of our existence. I haven't yet lost the bug for it. Not the wet and smelly organic but the stuff you can carry away and make into something new.

Typical of rural villages in the past before municipal waste services, Tàrbena had a rubbish tip about a kilometre and a half away on a bend on the spectacular mountain road. In such a beautiful place, it must have been horrible. The locals threw their waste off the cliff and down the mountainside. Amazingly, the growing pile was in full sight of the village.

I wonder what treasures lie below. For certain, there's material evidence of village life now buried under waving grasses and fan palms. We are our discarded rubbish. The story of a time and a place, sleeping on for now, an archaeological record in the making.

December 2017

Reaper Called

Sad the three notes
Tolled by the bell
The reaper had called
In the night on the hill
A soul passed on
From person to ghost
A sleep with no waking
Or maybe
It will

I asked in the square
Who? Do you know?
The hearse stood empty
Not a flower
Could be seen
As you reap shall you sow
Not of the village
Said Maggie who lives
In the town on the hill

Born here but went away
Where to
She just couldn't say
But back for this day
The church door opens
A priest said the words
Alone with the coffin
And perhaps
Someone's soul

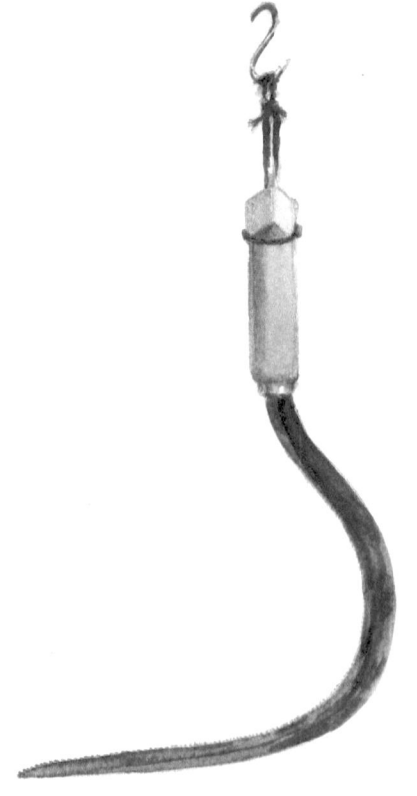

October 2017

There's No Smoke Without Firewood

January and it's chilly for here. It's serious when I start wearing socks with my sandals. Winter is having its little petulant flurries in the mountains. It's nothing in comparison with what the rest of Europe is experiencing. But enough for fires to be lit early and smoke to perfume the streets and alleys with the scent of apple, pear, olive, and almond wood burning in the grates. Wood gathered earlier in the year and stacked beneath the sun in the campo is collected, starting in September, and kept dry in the cellars beneath the houses.

Most of the old houses have cellars where, besides stabling for the mules and housing for the chickens, rabbits and pigs, there was a space allocated for storage and drying of winter fuel. These last few wintry days have been all about wood for the fire, for now and for the future. Wood is the preeminent fuel.

During the latter part of the year, you see tractor-trailer loads coming into the village, dumped next to a house then laboriously carried by hand in black *capazos* (rubber buckets) and down the steps into the cellars. This also happens in the winter months, because that's when the tree pruning is done.

Both our neighbours work the land. Sandwiched between them our house is co-joined with theirs. Beneath the houses there's a labyrinth of cellars, several of which are carved out of, or built into, the solid rock of the mountain.

As it's been cold enough to warrant a jacket to go out in, rather than warm ourselves with the thought that Spring is just around the corner, we decided to be prudent and get some more logs in. So off down the mountain, in our old car, we went to a woodyard on the outskirts of a town near to the coast.

We've been going there for a couple of years for our firewood. We know we're paying for heat and smoke, but realised a couple of years into living here, that a fifty-euro load of logs collected by us, transported by us, and offloaded by us, was better value than an eighty-euro (plus) trailer load from the local farmers.

The reason being that buying locally doesn't guarantee the fuel you're getting is dry and solid. That's not to say the locals are cheating. It's what they themselves have filled their trailers with after pruning and cutting down their trees for firewood.

There's something disappointing and annoying about picking up a large log you've bought as part of a load, which looked like it could run a power station for a week, then discovering the bark encloses a hollow interior in which various families of six-legged creatures and the odd snake or two have made a home.

To be fair, it's not all like that. But as we have discovered, at the wood yard, we pay fifty euros for a load of logs which fills the back of the car with solid oak or olive logs. It seems expensive, but from the wood yard, you get what you pay for. That load burnt in our wood stove will last us a month.

Our neighbour on our left-hand side, a lovely Dutch lady, resident here since God was a lad, works on the land. I was unloading the logs when she arrived home. She looked at the line of bags I was stacking before taking indoors. "You buy wood for the fire?"

"Yes."

She was curious about where they came from and how much they cost. I told her. She must have thought us crazy as she gets her firewood for free.

Our other neighbour on our right-hand side also works on the land. His house overlooks their land. He does the work of at least three men. This last week he's spent completing the winter task of pruning his almond trees. This, as a by-product, produces winter fuel for his parents' house. Logs are of various widths, but of the same length. He sorts and loads them into his trailer on the terraces and then hauls them back to his family's house. The length of the logs is important for he knows his cellar and the bay in which he'll stack the logs as well as the width of their stove. He has a corner fireplace that is massive, so he cuts his logs long. His family's house has built-in ducts that extend from the chimney of the wood burner, channelling the rising warm air into the rooms above. I wished someone had thought about that when renovating our house.

As he comes out of the valley below, his tractor must be reversed up the steep lane at the side of our houses, steering while looking backwards with the dexterity of a moon-lander pilot. Up it comes, the trailer stacked, slow and chugging, finally round the top right-angle bend (in reverse) and then down into the open mouth of the waiting cellar next to our front door. Once in, he unloads and stacks the first of several loads.

It's not wood that they'll burn during the remainder of this winter. No, it will rest there and dry during the cycle of the year, warm air entering through the barred windows, slowly drying the beautifully piled stack of fuel for next winter.

While he was in the business of collecting wood from his terraces below our houses, a small group of men arrived from the village council. They parked their flat-bed truck outside and descended the alley, recently climbed by our neighbour's redoubtable tractor. They were to clean up the remains of the therapeutic treatment of a magnificent date palm which grows below in the crook of the valley elbow.

There's a palm weevil about and it's attacking the palms. One treatment, drastic though it appears, is the hard pruning of the trunk and fronds. This left a pile of palm pieces, which in the mysterious ways of time in Spain had waited weeks to be cleared by the newly arrived gang.

Inside, our dog was barking furiously. I went to the door. The council chaps were carting up the remains of the pruning to load into the truck and take away to the village incinerator.

I still had some logs to bring into the house. One of the young men spotted them. He held up a palm frond at me. "*Para fuego?*"

"You mean for the fire? I asked.

"*Sí, claro,*" (yes, of course).

If we took the palm pieces, we'd save them a job of carting them, our house being 50 metres away from the tree.

"*Sí, gracias.*" They piled a stack by our front door. Suddenly, after purchasing ten bags of oak logs, we now had, in addition, a sizeable pile of palm tree, wet by recent showers, but when dry, combustible.

After bringing the first loads into our little house and down several flights of steps, on return to the surface, I discovered our farmer neighbour unloading his second trailer of logs, some of which were very large. For the first time, I heard him groan with effort. I'd almost finished and asked if I could help? But no, he didn't need help.

"You are a very kind man, thank you," he said in his best English.

I like to think that when I offer to help him, he doesn't think I'm nothing more than a feeble old man. Rather, he's proud and independent. Either that or he thinks I'd make a right cock-up of his lovely stack.

There's a sprinkle of icing sugar on the local mountains this morning, but nothing to get your thermals out of storage for. Our logs will see us through the cold weeks. As our lady farmer neighbour says, "Winter is almost over."

Adiós. I'll go and put another log on the fire.

January 2018

Dust

The main square, Plaça Major, in the middle of the village is the place where you almost always bump into someone you know. This day was no exception. Angela pointed behind her as she bustled by me heading towards the mini *supermercado*. "Dave's in the car."

He was sitting patiently inside with the windows open watching others and chatting to those who come near, unable now, without aid, to get out. I went to say hello. I like his sharp wit that says, I might be eighty-eight, but I've still got a brain!

"Where's Pascualet?" Dave knew Pascual well. The dog was born under a thorn bush near their house and grew up roaming freely among the terraces running with the flock. He often visited the homes scattered about where the residents gave him treats and lots of fuss. When Salvador sold his flock and retired, he gave the young dog to Dave and Angela, to their delight. Only weeks later, he wanted him back. The couple didn't know why, and never got over it. Pascual had become a member of the family. But what could they do?

"He's guarding the *casa*."

"Ah. The doctors told me I can't use the stairs anymore."

"Thank goodness you've got the ramp at the house."

Dave smiled. "Yes, it was good future planning, that."

They had built their mountain home from a ruin to their own design some years before. It stands secure on the rocky flank of a mountain surrounded by cacti and irises that Angela planted amongst the rocks. There's a broad terrace in front shaded by a venerable fig tree. Party tables with red chequered tablecloths complete the scene on summer days. The deep shadows between the tangle of dark boughs and branches above are thick with memories, like the sunbursts sparkling through the canopy, of glorious long hot afternoons with friends, with the Mediterranean below as a backdrop.

The mountainside falls steeply away beyond the garden. You can see the broken roofs of the ruined barn where Salvador sheltered his goats and where he dozed whilst his dogs, Pascual's mother and another, kept watch. Further down, the terraces of almond trees, pink in February, spread out like bridesmaids in a sun-filled church yard. Petal confetti blowing in the breeze. But no longer: The almonds have contracted a disease and are being destroyed.

Dave turned to speak again through the open window. His smile was gone and he was upset. "They've come and taken all the trees away. Forty almonds gone, forty!"

The week before, I saw a police car parked on a terrace beneath his house. They had come to guard against trouble from the almond growers who live hereabouts and who depend on the crop for their livelihood.

"Forty! Can you imagine?"

I nodded in agreement. "It's a desert now. Naked."

"Yes. When the rains come, it will wash away the soil. They're using a terrible machine. It makes great clouds of dust as it flattens the trees. Feels like we're living in hell when it was paradise."

I've seen the empty terraces myself. "There's craters where the trees were, like a battlefield."

"It used to be so beautiful," muttered the old gentleman wistfully. "Now, there's dust, only dust."

"Well, at least you've got the fig tree."

"Memories, lad," he said. "They'll soon be gone too."

January 2018

A Case of The Vapours

Today would have been a great day to steal a farm, a tractor, a car. Why not two? And a delightful home (the one you've always fancied). For the cloud has come down, or up, either way. It's already mid-February. It was almost too hot to linger on the terrace. Today has disappeared into veils of vaporised Mediterranean as thick as condensation on a post-shower mirror in that freezing flat you remember.

The cacti drip, translucent pearl lenses hang amongst the spikes. The dog's hairbrush, laced with filaments of dew looks like treasure on the old wooden table rescued from the dump. Terracotta tiles bejewelled with tiny aqua worlds, gems of liquid and light mysterious as oceans on distant planets.

On the spiral stairs, the steps ring like bells; water drips from the roof above. I listen, fascinated; a few notes ring out time and time again. It's a performance, more Stockhausen than damp weather.

Yesterday, all blinding brilliance, today, a peasouper. A cumulus nimbus came to call, floating pompously up the valley, halting earthbound creatures in their tracks, lost in its ballooning bosom.

The almonds, those which survived the cull, fresh blossomed pink, come in and out of sight on the mountainside, ghost bridesmaids at a cloud wedding where the photos were ruined by a breath of breeze and confetti too wet and sticky to fall.

And all around, the parched land, teased by light showers, yearns to drink the voluminous cloud which by tomorrow will have blown away and gone who knows where.

February 2018

Whiter Than White

Summer in the village is upon us, and so is the traditional fiesta, which the Spanish take seriously. Kath, several artist friends and I had been involved in setting up, managing, and running an art exhibition over the last few weeks. The show poster included a photo of a painting of mine, a pair of white socks pegged on a clothesline, behind them a brilliant blue sky with misty white-pink clouds. In the Spanish sun, colours are more intense, surreal actually. I titled the painting Whiter than White.

We created a pop-up gallery. The event, based in my small studio, spilled over to the outside walls and in the little-used open-air laundry right across from my door. The production has been a revelation. Not only of local talent but also of how beautiful the old laundry is, and what a unique exhibit it made. It was magical.

I like to paint. It thrilled me to discover that an old open outdoor laundry with no glass in the windows is a fabulous location in which to paint, a great big studio with water running through it. But, of course, it continues to be a laundry for the use of the villagers. The *lavadero* goes back a long way. It's not used much now, as people have washing machines. But twice I have been gob-smacked by events.

I was sitting there in the relatively cool afternoon air, painting away at my easel when a German couple, Ingrid and Peter who live in the *campo*, came in with great big buckets and bags of their laundry to wash.

We had covered the walls and ledges with paintings. Notwithstanding, they set to dunking, rubbing, wringing and rinsing out their smalls and sheets. It was like a "happening", an art performance.

As the pair got busy with their arms in the water, my farmer neighbour Pepe was outside managing the run-off *agua* to his plot below. He poked his face through the railings next to the couple to have words about them dunking their stuff.

I suppose he was worried that detergent might kill off his melons. I couldn't understand a word, and I supposed neither could they.

The lovely washer folks continued undeterred, scrubbing now without soap. I carried on painting, then after a few minutes, they filled their buckets with sopping washing and headed out, wishing me a good afternoon with a Northern European accent.

I tell you, dear reader, you can't make up better stuff than daily real life here.

This morning, two days left of the art exhibition, I went down to open the iron laundry gates. We planned a beautiful evening of candlelight, cold running spring water and lots of paintings. I was astonished to see that the crystal waters that flow through the trough from the mountain springs had become a cloudy white.

Washing detergent, I immediately thought, no!

I asked JC, the man from the council, about it. He said the water was murky because the street painters (villagers young and old decorate the streets every year on the eve of the fiesta) washed out their brushes in it. Of course, they did!

Adiós, from crazy, fabulous *fiesta* Tàrbena.

July 2018

A Crematorium and a Church

There was a funeral of a very special Yorkshireman here on our mountain.

The service in the charming church in Bolulla made me think of another such event. This time in a modern crematorium, which also marked the end of a Yorkshireman's life.

I remember a few years back, going with my elderly mum to a crematorium high on a windy hill on the East Yorkshire Wolds. The car park was as empty and stark as the winter trees were of leaves.

Inside, the nave-like space had seats for hundreds. It was vast, making us even more aware that we were the only people there.

Mum and I sat near the front, hand in hand, waiting for a coffin we couldn't see, to be consumed.

As the music we'd requested faded in and echoed around, we felt sad for Trevor. Not only for his passing, but also for the obvious fact that, apart from us, at the end, he was entirely alone.

Those empty rows spoke much of how he'd been regarded. I think that's why I cried.

How very different from the funeral of a much-loved fellow, on Monday September 17, 2018.

Instead of a vacant hall on a windy hill, the beautiful medieval church of Bolulla, a thousand feet down from our village, was packed to overflowing. Local Spanish and English family members and a multitude of expats and other friends; they'd all come to say a final goodbye to an extraordinary and well-loved man. Hundreds of people, there to pay their last respects to Gentle Dental Dave.

Why was the church filled that way? Because David meant something special to all and each. Fond loving memories were being replayed in each head. Thousands of thoughts in many languages, spinning his soul into animation again as his coffin was wheeled by to the accompaniment of voices singing in unison. He was quite altruistically gifted. He adjusted dentures, mended broken teeth, and generally helped people smile with confidence again. After his funeral, an elderly Bolulla woman approached me and, pointing to her mouth said, "You see this smile of mine? David did that for me. He was a good man."

It made me realise—judge not only how a man lived, and what he achieved, but, at his mortal end, how those he touched regarded him.

My memory of him was of good humour and humanity, and of course, of him standing on our front step in the village, come to fix me a temporary tooth for a TV interview back in Britain. Smiling as always, his freckled hand shook as he held his trusty battery powered DIY drill.

September 2018

Dental Dave and the Mystery of the Telly Tooth

Tàrbena, our village, used to be far more isolated than it is now. Even today it can feel remote, mainly because the road to get here on both sides of the mountain is steep and winding. Back in the early eighties, so we're told, there wasn't a continuous road. And neither was there a dentist, which meant a lot of toothaches and broken dentures.

Dave, retired Master Dental Technician, originally came from the Yorkshire seaside town of Scarborough. He lived in two villages in the mountains (not at the same time). One was Bolulla, lower down the mountain, where he lived for twenty years and up here, just outside Tàrbena, in a house he and his wife Angela converted from a ruined stone barn with a beautiful view down to the sea.

Having a heart as big as Yorkshire, Dave would help people out by fashioning and fitting missing teeth and dentures, and became, through so doing, a hero of the people.

I'll never forget that it was Dave and his wife who introduced us to their daughter Helen, who has a house here. We ended up renting it. Today I keep my studio/workshop there.

Back then, we weren't sure after moving in whether the local Spanish villagers would accept us. But with Dave as a friend, we had the best possible ambassador to introduce us and break the ice.

Soon after we'd moved in, he came to visit us, to see how we were. After his visit, I walked up the hill towards the centre of the village with him.

As we talked our way up Calle San Miguel, an old lady dressed in black came towards us. As she got close enough to make the figure out as him, she flung open her arms and embraced him enthusiastically. I thought, it must be his aftershave.

After he could prise himself away, he turned to me and said proudly the immortal words, "I fixed her dentures."

I was gob smacked by how very popular he was and how friendly the locals were towards him. I remember thinking, when you come to a place like this as an outsider, you don't only take, you give. That's what Dave did. After a while of knowing him, I realised that when he saw someone in the village he was thinking, "Back right 23 apposite impacted" (or whatever dental people say).

So, going back to 2014, early in the year. I had my first book coming out and had planned to visit the UK, Yorkshire and York specifically, to do a bit of promotion for it and the Jorvik Viking Centre, for which I designed the exhibitions. I also, like the old folks of Tàrbena, had a problem: a big hole in my smile, a missing tooth.

"I could fix that for you if you are desperate," said Dave one day in the local bar.

"You could?!"

"Why didn't you have the missing front row tooth fixed before? Makes you look like a hillbilly."

"Thanks."

"No," he said, checking himself and looking more closely. "Makes you look like a poverty struck idiot."

"So kind."

I explained why it was a problem to have the tooth replaced with an implant.

"No matter, I can fix it.

"That would be great because I've got to do an interview with Harry Gration on BBC telly, North at Six. They want to talk about the 30th anniversary celebration of the opening of Jorvik and my book. I was the Project Designer of the first one and I wrote a book about it. I can't wear a bag on my head for that."

"True. It would be temporary though. The tooth not the bag."

"Well," now extremely self-conscious of the horrible hole in the front of my face, "if you could fix me up so I could do some press photos and that telly interview, it would be wonderful! It wouldn't have to last forever. Then I could go back to being an idiot."

A few days later, after coming first to take measurements, colour matches, casts, that sort of thing, and then making the tooth, he arrived at our door.

I went to let him in. Usually when you opened the door to Dave, it was like the sun was shining in. But not that morning. It was as if the inquisition had arrived.

"I've come to do the installation," he said, smiling his Scarborough smile.

I looked in horror, not at him, rather at what he was carrying. In his hand was a small Dremel, a power drill. His hands were shaking. I stood to block the door so he couldn't get in.

"Aren't you going to let me in?" He sounded a bit hurt and his hand holding the drill shook even more.

"You're not putting that thing in my mouth! No way! I'd rather go on telly without a head."

"That's not going anywhere close to your mouth. It's for polishing and such."

"Oh, come in then."

"Righto. You're doing the Beeb interview in eleven days? What was the UK time of the interview? So, you'd be done, what, about 6:20-ish?" He was taking notes.

Jump forward to April 2014. Dave installed the tooth the day before we left for the UK. For the first time in a long while, I felt okay to smile, laugh and act relatively normally instead of keeping my big mouth closed and growing a moustache down to my chin.

We were in Yorkshire over a week, and now was the day of the BBC North interview in Leeds. Dave's false tooth was firmly and securely in my front row. I had had strict instructions before leaving to lay off toffee, anything that needed biting and refrain from opening beer bottles with my teeth. Thank God he said nothing about pulling corks.

And so came the day of the interview.

I sat on the sofa in the studio being interviewed and felt the confidence of knowing I could smile at the book-buying public. I was so confident by now of Dave's mountain molar masterwork in my mouth, that I didn't think about it.

After a few minutes of BBC exposure, we were out and about to leave the studios. It was all over. Kathy was waiting for me off camera and I joined her.

"Phew. Glad that's done. Let's go and have a glass of wine."

We were approaching the main exit door when something in my head went PING! To my astonishment, out of my mouth and onto the tiles below popped my false tooth. "I don't believe it! What time is it?"

Kath looked at her watch. "It's 6:20 pm. Right on time!"

Bless him. He'll be fixing the dentures of angels now. I'm sure he is.

April 2014

The Thing

A thing arrived at our house. A man in a uniform brought a box and couldn't get away fast enough. The gadget looks like something from *Back to the Future*, has the personality of a Dalek from *Doctor Who* and the appetite of a wild elephant. The object doesn't stop eating. We have to feed it constantly or we're sure it will turn its glassy eyes on us.

The device is in the kitchen now in a corner, proceeding to eat us out of house and home. As soon as it was out of the box, it consumed an armful of celery by teatime. This morning, I found my wife trying to placate the dastardly little thingamajig with apples, plums, peaches, and yet more celery. Thank God it's vegetarian (so far). It would have the Bratwursts out of the fridge and Pascual's chicken leftovers, and come to think of it, the dog as well.

The gadget growls and grinds and has lights that flash and it constantly excretes sludge and opaque liquids. Then (by thought control) makes us drink it.

The thing cost an arm and a leg, weighs more than our dog, and looks like it's here to stay. Hang on, where *is* Pascual? I ask my wife the knower of things; what shall we feed it when there's nothing left. Don't look at me!

September 2018

End of an Era

A couple of evenings ago, my wife and I returned home to find three tired looking men in overalls sitting on the bench outside our front door. They'd been working on the land for hours and were drinking beer and wine. I got the impression they were happy to have finished their labours.

While Kath went inside, eager to unpack her basket of garden produce from her allotment, the younger fellow motioned me to join them. I fetched a couple of cans of *cerveza* (beer) and joined them.

The older fellow the other two had been working for was a *bombero*, a fireman, in one of the large cities on the coast. A man of great energy and pride, he seemed tired and dejected. Flattened.

I paused before the one who was our neighbour. "A good day?"

"No, a bad day," he said, shaking his head.

"*Lo siento*," I replied in my awful accent. "I feel for you."

"It is finished, over, done."

"What, no more harvesting to do?" I thought he was referring to the day's task.

"No, the whole thing, it is ended. The trees are dry, and the almonds are not worth picking."

"You mean they have the disease?" His trees fill the valley below. A disaster.

"Yes. It is over," he declared with an air of finality.

"But your land and all those years, what…?"

"I am lucky. It is not my job."

I looked at the other men. It was theirs. What future for them?

Somehow, I had thought our neighbour's almond trees would escape the terrible plague that had caused so many trees to die. But no. For all his work around the year, for all his care. For all his free time away from his profession, spent on the mountain labouring in the *campo* that his family have owned and farmed for generations. It was over.

"I am so sorry."

"Don't be. I am lucky. I have a job."

October 2018

Pascual's Tale

Having a studio at the entrance of the village with a large, raised garage door has its advantages. The main one being, I interact with people who pass by. I have stuff I like to put on display, paintings and walking sticks made from local wood. If they're curious enough, they'll come down the ramp from the road. They take in the gurgling font in the yard, cautiously pass the sleeping dog (who's got one eye open), then peek inside my converted garage to see what I'm up to. I never know who may show up.

I meet people and their dogs when I'm walking in the campo too. Mostly you don't run into another soul, but when you do, you always say hello and pass the time of day.

There's an area close to our village that Pascual and I walk, one of our favourite routes. Even though we might go that way twice a week, to him it is always new, yet he knows it as well as the back of his paw.

I love paths and being out on them as much as he does. We never tire of them even though we tread them frequently. We know them intimately. The mountain landscape is stunning, jaw-dropping sometimes. The paths through it are fascinating; they tell stories, like the lines on a lived-in face or long-worked hands. You can read them as you follow them if you have a curious eye and an open ear. But watch where you step; those interesting rocks and turns, steps and drops can trip you; donkeys and mules had four feet!

Animals which could tolerate, thrive, and labour in such challenging wild landscapes, especially in the summer heat, left their signature upon it. They would have walked and worn the smooth limestone rocks, which now shine, polished over centuries by hooves and sandals. There's a network of venerable pathways all over the landscape, although it is not always evident now. They were an essential part of life, with no proper roads. One track leads from the village two thousand feet down the mountain to the next village below and on to the coast twenty-five kilometres away. On it, decades ago, surplus products produced here or special to the area would have been transported by mule and traded.

On one of my best loved walks, it's always good to stop and grab your breath for a minute and look to the east; the vista is absolutely gobsmacking. The Costa Blanca stretches out before you, framed by mountains on each side. With its backdrop of the Mediterranean and matching clear blue sky, it's as though you're on a balcony looking down on a giant stage.

The path I'm thinking about is hard work but great exercise. The rocky trail up is challenging. There's another route, a narrow single-track concrete road leading to grand houses, second homes of well-off people who most of the year live elsewhere.

Pascual must have had a previous connection with a palatial house at the top of the hill. When we get up there, if he's off the lead, he runs into the garden as though he owned the place.

Indeed, the way he runs in with such certainty and anticipation has convinced me he lived another life there; it was a homecoming for him. This happens in other spots on this side of the peak. We don't know much about his past. On walks in the surrounding hills, he'll suddenly pick up a scent or recognise the view that triggers memories (I believe dogs have memories, not solely associations). His whole being appears to brighten with pleasure. We grew accustomed to living with this mysterious creature and wanted to uncover his history, to understand why no one who knew him had adopted him. His provenance was everywhere; everyone had their own story about him. All the natives greeted him by the name they'd given him, Pascualet, with such warmth. He was a loved and respected gentleman, not a semi-wild mountain dog who in those early months of our ownership scared Kath and me half to death. He was the resident with roots; we were the incomers who barely existed. When the locals acknowledged him with a warm *hola*, most times they ignored us. Not even a glance.

The way things happened around the time we adopted him made me feel we may have been well and truly setup. We now owned a legendary animal, we were his keepers, and carers, and possibly not up to the job. We had saved him from the dogs' home and, most likely, euthanasia.

After several months, when he behaved better, and we hadn't given up on him, or been too frightened to have him share our small home, things changed. For when crossing the village square, locals acknowledged us too, no names at first, only a nod of recognition, but they called out "Pascualet" with a smile. They started commenting in the local language how good he looked. The old men who sat on their sunny step in front of the church on the square no longer appeared to be taking bets on which of us would lose our fingers or nose and stopped sniggering into their sleeves as we passed.

He had a heritage as bright as a painted saint. We had given Pascualet a second chance at life. People loved him and respected him, making him an object of pride that they all shared. They were glad he'd stayed alive after Salvador, his shepherd owner, had died.

We became more curious. Why did he have the sort of reputation he had? Bit by bit, piece by piece from locals and expats, we understood.

I met Desiree in my studio one summer shortly after we had adopted Pascualet. I connected with her immediately when she walked in. She was as smart as she was gorgeous and literally made my knees wobble. I could feel my earlobes glowing. If I'd been single, and she not accompanied by a two-meter-tall godlike Norseman called Olaf the Destroyer, I would have given him a run for his thunder.

Desiree is Norwegian and was on holiday from her career as a judge, staying at the residence of her uncle, who is also a judge. The large dwelling high on the hill overlooking the village is partly visible from my studio window. She lit up when she saw Pascual asleep in the sawdust at the back. It was almost as if she had encountered an old friend.

She knew him because he used to come to the house, but, that day, she didn't have time for further explanation since Thor was hankering after a pint of lager, but she promised to tell me more when they next passed by.

Later I met her uncle, Balland, who claimed he knew Pascual when the dog ran with Salvador's goats. He looked like an old goat himself, unkempt hairy chin, wild thin hair, don't-care wrongly buttoned shirt revealing grey on a concave chest. Though he seemed to be a down-and-out, he was obviously anything but. Rather, as I soon realised, he was an ageless human dynamo.

I told Kathy about the meeting. "What a coincidence. Why not ask him if you could interview him? You want to write a book about Pascual. He could give you all the details of his younger life that you'll no doubt need for it."

She was right. This was a golden opportunity if I was serious about writing it.

During a walk, I recognised Balland outside his house when he came for one of his stays. I asked if he would be willing to be interviewed for this book I want to write called *The Last Shepherd's Dog*. As he eagerly agreed to the suggestion, Kath, Pascual, and I trekked up to his palatial holiday home. It was Friday, August 19, Pascual's birthday, or so we believed.

We arrived at Balland's after a 30-minute trek up the hill. It supposedly being Pascual's birthday made this visit extra momentous.

Our host stood at the wrought-iron gate at the side of the house. He'd heard the panting and pausing as we crawled up the hot concrete track. Once again, he didn't look like the holder of a spectacularly grand dwelling; obviously age and means were his dressers. He came over to greet the three of us on the terrace, making us feel at home. Pascual, off his lead, recognised and ran to him. We looked on as they made a mutual fuss.

The gentleman showed us in, where the cool vaulted space through the gate felt like a cave beneath the mountain. From the hallway we walked down the broad unlit corridor with daylight at the far end. We turned an abrupt left into a great long room with arched windows flanking the other side. Curtains moved softly, framing and re-framing the view of the bleached haze of the coast. The spacious, shady area was pleasant after our scorching walk up.

"Please sit," he directed in a Norwegian accent. Pascual explored the terrace and beyond.

"Do you mind?"

"No, there's nothing here for him apart from memories."

Our eyes soon became adjusted to the darkness. Paintings appeared on the walls, landscapes, seascapes, relatives, all beautifully portrayed. Then we returned to the brilliance of the noon light.

From the huge balcony outside, as open and wide as a Broadway stage, we took in the broad vista. As we picked and pointed, oohed and aahed at the view, Pascual ran about freely, panting heavily. Balland offered us ice cold glasses of lemonade and Kath asked for a bowl of water for the dog.

Pascual was obviously excited to be there. Who says dogs don't have memories? He seemed to be checking them off a list. Fascinatingly, his curiosity was not all about potential sources of food or treats; he was reliving the place and returning home. He was familiar with it and was searching not for things, but for people.

We stayed out on the balcony and, to avoid the intense sun, our host showed us to a shady corner around a small circular coffee table where we could do the interview. Pascual stretched out on the cool tiles and fell asleep, remaining unimpressed, as though he'd heard it all before.

I was curious about the size and design of his house. In Norway all houses outside the big cities are made of wood."

"When did you first come here before you met the dog?"

"As far back as 1984, that's when I began to visit, though rarely. I was very busy. I would say I visited every four to five years. My cousin, who owned the house, got stomach cancer, and had to quit the project. By then it was almost complete, so it was even more galling for him, so near yet so far. He became critically ill. I bought it from him when he lost interest and could not finish it. Sadly, in 2004 he died."

I flipped open my notebook. "So, what are your first memories of Pascualet? I know you had another name for him."

"I recall when he came into the world." He stood up and pointed over and down below the parapet. "He was born under that thorn bush down there."

"He grew up here, one of many puppies. The mother of Pascualet, she was always pregnant. When this one here was born in the bushes, the puppies found their way up to and into the house. Of course, they were helpless babies, and their mother was off goat-herding without them, so they had to fend for themselves. We gave them food and water; my wife melted when they turned up at the door. Salvador had some rooms down there in the fold building and often stayed overnight. In the morning, he made his way out with the goats and the adult dogs early before the heat switched on. The puppies and very young dogs couldn't follow on the mountainsides among all the rocks and cacti, so they looked after themselves, and spent their daytimes here with us."

"What fortunate dogs!" I said.

He looked off into the distance. "I don't remember how many, five or six. They were shepherd dogs or in training and they all followed him; he was their pack-leader, it was natural for them. Pascual, when he grew up, became one of the working pack that trailed Salvador and the goats out in the campo every day."

"That was his mother's life as well, among the herding dogs?" Kath asked.

"She was the boss dog; no man or beast messed with her if you wanted to keep your face! And no other adult or adolescent dog dared to challenge her. She was ferocious and let nothing pass."

I was intrigued. "So, that's where Pascual gets his spirit from, his mum!"

"When Salvador stopped work and sold the goats, he moved permanently to the village and left the mother of your dog by herself on the mountain. Salvador, even though he had so many of them, dogs, and goats, he was not very attentive to animals. He didn't care. They were like machines to him, doing a job. Apart from occasionally, when there would be one he favoured.

"After moving to the village, he left the dogs to look after themselves. Let's be straight about this: those animals had a tough life, they had to take care of themselves. It was like reverting to the wild for them. They had to add to whatever food he doled out to them from wherever else they could get it."

Pascual woke up, glanced our way, then slumped back down.

"Did the other dogs look like him?" Kath asked.

"No, his mother only. His mother looked like him."

"We saw her when Jorge brought us to his farm to collect him when we first took him for a weekend try out." I recalled that visit vividly.

"I thought that was his father," Kath said.

This tickled Balland. "No, nobody knows who he was!"

"So, his mother was a big dog?" Kath was in full interviewer mode now.

"Yes, very much like him, perhaps a little larger. I think I have a picture of her. Wait, maybe it's here in these." He'd earlier produced an assorted collection of aging colour prints. "Oh, I didn't print it out. Darn. She's not here."

"Was she beautiful?"

"Oh yes, very. Even though she lived a hard life and had to fight for so much, she remained beautiful."

"He's very handsome." Kath glanced over at Pascual as if he were a baby in a cot. As she did so, I saw him lift an ear. I swear he knew we were talking about him and loved every minute of attention.

I had another question. "But if you came and went as you did, you caught only brief glimpses of their lives?"

"Yes, yes. Of course, we stayed for a few weeks at a time. I never lived here permanently. Only for vacation, but when here you couldn't resist becoming attuned to the activity nearby in the campo and on the mountain. A graphic example, once the men who work here set up traps in the bushes for the wild boars, the *jabalí*. One morning I came out and heard (he makes the sound of a crying dog). And this one," he points to Pascual, "one trapped him, choking him around the neck." Pascual looked at Balland.

"When I came across him, it had almost strangled him. So, I saved him from that trap. Then a few days later, we couldn't see him, we were worried about him. The mother was here (he makes sounds of a crying dog), and she acted very restless. She knew something was wrong with him. We could tell something was not right. For three days we didn't see him. We shouted the name we had given him, Bruno, but no response. We couldn't understand it. Early one morning, we were leaving for Norway. So, we started in the car at 7 o'clock. I have the valve for the tap water for the house on the footpath on the hill. So, I had to stop my car down where the houses finish… down there on the road. I walked up to turn off the valve when I heard a dog barking, in the hill here. We drove back, and I used my ears and walked on the *bancales*. There he was again in another trap—for three days! And this time he had it around his ankle here."

"Was it this leg?" Kathy points to Pascual's rear right leg.

"Yes, the trap injured that one."

We'd noticed early on he was very sensitive there and that his ankle twists as he steps. But it doesn't stop him from running and jumping.

Balland lowered his head. "He had been there for three days."

I was appalled by the thought. "Bloody hell."

"Fortunately, we had ample time. So, we took him to the house and gave him water and food."

"You rescued him. If it hadn't been for you, he probably would have lost his leg."

"Oh yes, he may have died from injury and blood loss."

"Was he a puppy, or older?" Kathy asked.

"I cannot remember his exact age. Must have been two or three years old. Fully grown, I would say."

Kath looked down at our prepared list of questions and asked him what year he first encountered him as a pup.

"I cannot tell you, no sorry. Because the time passes here quickly for us. We stay here two, three or four times every year. So, it's impossible to say."

Kath was hoping to verify his birthdate. "His passport says he was born August 19, 2008. He's 14 years old this year."

"That may be correct. Who has stated that? Salvador? He wouldn't write it down, I'm sure."

Kath explained that we weren't positive, and Pascual's start in life was a mystery as well. We thought he'd been born on that day in 2008 based on the official *Certificación* that accompanied his pet passport, although the passport itself stated it was the date he was micro-chipped, which wouldn't have been done on the day he was born. Which was it? To our knowledge, he was 14 years old now. People who knew him as a puppy assumed so too.

"Do you know Helen? Angela and David? Angela's daughter Helen, they lived in the house directly above the goat shed," I said.

"Oh yes, yes. I didn't know him, but I met him once."

"They were very close to Pascual. He used to visit them in 2008, they are certain. They have photographs too." Kath leaned forward. "Do you know what's funny? You called him Bruno. Angela and David named him Charley."

"Stewart and Jenny, our friends who live over there..." I pointed to their house on the steep slope of the adjacent hill... "they also called him Charley. He visited them too; we've discovered he had a whole routine of visits to make. He was too smart to go hungry. I don't think he cared what people called him."

"I'll tell you why we called him Bruno, because Salvador had another favourite, more poodle like. He was totally white. His name was Blanco, yes, it's Spanish, Blanco. And this one here he was not white, but brown. In Norwegian, *brun* is the word for brown. The other dog was Blanco because he was white and then we named him Bruno because he was brown."

"When did your wife become so attached to him?" I asked.

"She has always been fond of animals, cats, and dogs. She cares very much... and the other day when I met you down at the swimming pool, I took a photo of him."

I went back to our list of questions. "Back in those days, as a young dog, did Pascualet possess any individual quality, something that showed in the way he reacted to things? Did he seem to be expressive of a personality?"

"No, I cannot say that. He was one of a pack. Sometimes Salvador had five at once. It was only when he had a specially favoured dog, that was a black poodle named Linda, who stayed with him in the house first. The rest were workers. Later, when that dog died, he adopted this one (he points to Pascual) to live with him in the house. He stayed with Salvador in the village for several years before Salvador died."

Kath spoke up. "Helen told us Angela and David kept him for a while. They took him in as he roamed about after Salvador retired. After a while, Salvador came to David and said he wanted him back!"

Balland nodded. "That's possible."

"You told me the other day a moving story about how you were going up or down in the village. You had seen Pascual and his mother reunited on San Miguel Street?"

"Yes, I can't tell you the year. He was staying with Salvador, who left the mother out on the terrain. She stayed with us when we came here. This mother, he left her to herself. She stayed down there at the goat shed. As long as we stayed here, she lived with us. She was old and lived only a little while. One day, we would take our daily trip around the hill there. We used to go into the terrain and return up to Pelut's Restaurant. The other dog followed us on the street that morning. She came right back with us all the time. Suddenly, down in the street, Salvador came against us. You should have seen the meeting when this one and his mother met. Oh, that was so touching.

"But afterwards she followed us and went back to her place on the mountain." Balland paused, delving deep into his memory. "First, they stood on the back street caring for each other and then they stopped like this to do some playing around."

"They recognised one another?" said Kath.

"And joy yeah, I am sure of it." He looked through the photos and produced two. "Here's my wife making food for the dogs. There's Blanco, and there's Linda, the mother of this dog."

We looked at the photo. "Gosh, she's so similar. They're like twins."

"Twins, yes."

"Oh, my goodness gracious. It's amazing! They are so alike!" said Kath. "Is that unusual, a mother and her son so alike?"

"I will take this picture, make a copy and mail it to you," offered Balland.

Kath held the photo down to Pascual's face; he opened his eyes. "You look exactly like your mummy!"

"Can we share our plans for the book?" I asked.

Kath explained. "Before we had Pascual we lived in Helen's house, the daughter of Angela, on Calle San Miguel."

"Where my studio is," I clarified.

"We would walk up San Miguel. Salvador must have recently retired from his flock and changed his residence to the village. We used to see Pascualet galloping up the street from here toward the Plaza. I remember the first time I saw him, I thought, what a beautiful dog. He was running, as he does, and he looked at me but wouldn't stop. He's not a dog that engages with people. We had heard a story from another villager, Erik, and his wife, Esperanza. They owned an Alsatian bitch a few years ago. When she came into heat, Pascual climbed a three-metre chain-link fence to get to her and got her pregnant."

Balland burst out laughing.

"Erik said that the thing that struck him was that the dog had the energy to climb up, and down, perform, and then climb back out! Erik swears that, although he witnessed the event, he can hardly believe it even now."

I asked, "Was that the incident where someone filed a complaint, *denuncia*, after which Salvador had to keep him on a lead?"

"A rope it was. He used to pull Salvador around on the end of it!" He picked up another photo from the folder. "And this is his mother again."

"Oh, this is quite wonderful, Balland." I was as excited as if someone had opened a treasure chest.

Kath looked at more photos. "This big poodle-like one, was that Salvador's favourite dog at the time?"

"No. This one died here in my house. I cared for him. I put him in the bathtub and washed him. My God, he was in a terrible state, full of insects, ticks. He didn't care for his animals; it was the way it was."

"But he must have fed them?"

"Yes, he must have, but he was not good at looking after them always."

I remembered something. "I was at the swimming pool bar once when I saw Salvador feed Pascualet half of a full-size sandwich. I am sure it had sausage in it. Pascualet had my attention, so I watched. It amazed me at how quickly he gulped it down his throat."

Balland refilled our glasses. "Well, he must have fed them. But he didn't keep dogs in his house. They lived a semi-wild life and slept in a place for them in the goat house, under that collapsed roof down there. What kind of food I don't know."

I asked, "When Salvador returned to the village to sleep in his home, or go to the bar, did he shut the dogs in there, or leave them to...?"

"No, no, he did not shut them in. They roamed freely, but they stayed pretty much where the goats were. They knew it was their home."

Kath looked at her notes again. "So, can you tell us any more about his birth?"

"Yes. One day, we took a walk. My wife stopped, 'Listen, listen.' We heard noises from tiny puppies (he makes puppy whining sounds). 'It's coming from in that thicket,' my wife said. It was so full of thorns that no adult dogs apart from their mother would attempt to get in. The bush protected them."

"But could they get out?"

"They could get out, they were small. But I think that Mother Nature's instinct kept them there in the nest. Their mother would feed them, of course, the thorns wouldn't stop her. Her instinct prompted her to brave anything to care for them."

Kath asked, "Did you see the goats and sheep?"

"Oh yes, of course. Salvador always came along past here. We treated him like a friend. He was a likeable man, and we had a custom with him to come in for a beer, or a cognac. He was very fond of cognac."

Kath again, "Did he care for both sheep and goats? I've got different stories about what animals he tended in his flock."

"Yes, I think earlier he had both, but in the last ten to fifteen years he had only goats. They were more comfortable to work with. The sheep, they're more wild animals, in a sense. So, tell me, how did he come to be with you two?"

I recounted the story about how we each had seen Pascual running in the streets. "We preferred a little terrier. There were several terriers in the village. Then Salvador died. We didn't know him except to smile and nod to in the square. He would smile and nod back, but that was as far as it got. Often, we'd see them on the street where we live, Pascual on a rope, front legs in the air, pulling Salvador as he walked him, barely able to restrain him, as strong as Salvador was. But that was it."

I related how Álvaro offered to give us one of his pregnant terrier's puppies who would be born in a few weeks. And then our encounter with Javier at the burial of Salvador in the cemetery.

"Ha, different. They had set you up?"

"That's what it felt like, with good intention, though. But there was no comparison between a puppy terrier and a mountain shepherd dog in the prime of life."

Balland chuckled at that. "Yes, a little different."

"So, we decided that we'd have a weekend trial. Pascual knew because he was as good as gold on the lead. Do you remember Kath?"

"It was the opposite, John. He was very hyper, tense, bouncing as though electricity was going through his feet. He was extremely upset, possible separation anxiety because of Salvador's death, left in the house with the body for two days we heard."

"Yes." Balland had heard the same sad story.

"One thing I noticed about him," Kath said. "We've seen pictures of him with Salvador. He was so devoted; he had to be by his side, always."

"Salvador was his alpha."

Kath and I recounted all we went through once we took Pascual in. I shook my head. "We both knew it wouldn't be easy. The short story is we finally adopted him. The first three months turned out to be absolute hell. We nearly gave him up. He acted like a wild animal in the house."

"He wouldn't settle with you?"

"No, not at first. It was terrible. It was also ironic and funny." I told him too many times friends were dropping in and how Kath wanted a break from it. We got that break once Pascual came to live with us.

Balland found that amusing. "It must have been difficult."

"I had nightmares. I would come into the house from a walk with him. As I stood at the sideboard taking off my jacket, he'd jump up all the way up here...." Kath tapped the back of her neck.

"He felt he got a new home and that they were intruders," Balland said.

I looked over at Pascual lying quietly on the floor. "Yes, that's it. To this day, there are few people who will come to the door to deliver. He can be terrifying. He's older and more placid now, but he retains his reputation and a full set of teeth, and he knows how to intimidate. Ah, he's got worse again lately. Now that he doesn't hear or see very well."

Balland slapped his knee. "Same with me!"

"Old men. He's 96 in human terms," I said.

"And his hind legs are collapsing under him as well." Kath stroked Pascual's head.

"Instead of the pet we imagined, it was like managing a monster," I said.

"What happened? He calmed down?" asked Balland.

"What happened was actually what happened to us." I recounted our training sessions in Jávea. And that we were the ones being trained. "There's an English saying, 'Be careful what you wish for.' We had wished for a quieter time. We suddenly had silence apart from the crazy bark of a ferocious dog."

Kath rolled her eyes. "No more visitors dropping in unexpectedly."

"It's still like that. People are cautious; but they all love him as well now."

Kath checked her notes. "One last question, Balland. Do you think the villagers are afraid of him?"

"No, I don't think so. I couldn't think why."

"They've seen him fight with other dogs. He could be ferocious," I said.

"Of course, he is a powerful dog. All dogs can be dangerous if they feel they are in danger."

Kath closed her notebook. "Thank you so much. I can't tell you how valuable this has been to us."

"Is this the end? If so, would you like a proper tour of the house?"

"Yes please, we would, wouldn't we, Kath?"

"Absolutely!"

Balland stood up, stretched, and looked around. "Now, where is that lovely old dog? BRUNO! Ah, there he is."

Our dog came tearing round the corner, skidding to a halt on the tiles, fire and joy in his laughing eyes.

August 2022

The Beautiful Time

I remember those days in England in early autumn when we had been back in school for a couple of weeks, as damp leaves tumbled past the classroom window. The start of the rugby season and the cold shower room. How the daylight shortened, and the dark grew thicker, gnawing away at the edges of the day. The conkers brown and shining out of their shells and that earthy smell as you kicked up the leaf litter. The first fires in the hearth and smoke reluctant to climb the chimney and forays with other kids collecting whatever would burn for the coming bonfire of November fifth, Guy Fawkes Night.

Cast your mind back to the warm, balmy days when you would sweat on the playing field. Indian Summer, wondering what kind of Indians, and would you be having curry for tea?

And granddad's pipe smell mixing with the aromas of the end of season garden as he tidied it up for the winter.

October was always the in-between space, between that endless midsummer and the inevitable cold and dark to come, light enough to see your way to school and back home.

October and November on the Costa Blanca of Spain can be a mellow afterglow of summer; peaceful and comfortable. Visitors gone. Some days, the village is silent. Meanwhile, the sun illuminates everything with a sharpness. Oblique rays shine with a light that penetrates and illuminates from inside, revealing the bones of the familiar landscape.

What a wonderful time to walk. The countryside sharper yet pastel shaded, mountains basking in soft blues, purples, and pinks. The streets etched, shadows raven black, details revealed like a new pop-up version of itself.

At this turn of year, people no longer hide from the sunlight; they bathe in it. The senior men in front of the church venture out from the pool of shadow beneath the trees. The sun doesn't steal away energy in October; it enhances it.

It's the harvesting season. Tick-tack-tock of the workers' long canes amongst the almond branches up on the hills, the cornflake crunching of the shelling machine.

The blasted mosquitos, hungry and persistent are living on borrowed time, I am pleased to say. I tell them that every time I get bitten.

In our garden, as the heat diminishes, and the sun becomes kinder, a second spring arrives. Plants wake up. This is their chance for another shot at life before the cold comes to the mountain.

Juan and Canela often walk with me and Pascual. We never stop babbling on. He's an encyclopaedia of all things to do with the history and heritage of the village. Because of that, I call him Juan Who Knows.

I ran into him in the plaza this morning. "Hasn't the weather been grand lately?"

"Yes, it has. It's the beginning of the beautiful time."

October 2018

Pascual and The Lord of the Kingdom of the Mountains

The adventure Pascual and I had one morning was right up there on the list of never to be forgotten events.

Barbary Sheep, known locally as the *arruí*, have recently appeared in the area over the summer. We have had encounters several times, always fleeting, as well as seeing them on the hill above our house. They are magnificent creatures, wild as the wind, and can live up to 14 years or more; their only natural predators (of their infants) are Golden Eagles and foxes, both of which we have around us.

The rams weigh as much as 125 kilos and they grow amazing curving ribbed horns, hugely impressive. Their fur is a golden brown with black markings. To see a herd, wild and free, is an extraordinary experience. There they are, thriving in an arid landscape which supports them and provides all they need. Originating from the North African mountains, introduced to Spain to be hunted, they hop about on sheer rock faces as easily as if they were checking shelves in a shopping mall.

Having lived here a few years, walking in the local campo every day with my dog, I feel sad sometimes at how little wildlife there seems to be. That, of course, apart from the ubiquitous wild boar who could thrive in an underground carpark if they had to. So, what happened to Pascual and me that morning, so close to home, is even more meaningful and memorable.

A steep track from the village leads up to the top of the hill. It's a dramatic spot, a crest of limestone flanked by 900 plus metre peaks on either side and spectacular views down to the coast 25 kilometres away. The flanking mountains create a theatrical vista, with the Mediterranean Sea as a backdrop.

It's a favourite ramble of ours. We even have a name for it, The Up and Over Walk. This is a quick orientation guide: directly behind our little house in the valley, you ascend six hundred feet up an achingly steep causeway to the top. Only athletes would go up without pausing. The art in making the ascent pleasurable is to count twenty paces, then pause nonchalantly, half revolve your elegant walking stick describing an arc as you find a new anchor point to lean on. Then raise your head and take in the magical scene of village roofs and misted mountains. Wait for a few seconds as oxygen finds its way into your legs, then turn back and resume your climb. Now that Pascual is also an old man, he does the same thing, only he doesn't have a stick.

Having recovered our breath, me panting as loudly as him, we do the last bit of the ascent. The very top, where it flattens off, is our reward for the effort. The scene which unfolds in that space as you walk on is timeless and beautiful, with spectacular mountains now appearing on the horizon.

We reach an enchanted place, a grove of great-great-great grandparent olive trees. Ancient, all seeing, and all knowing; my thoughts whisper in my head in their presence. They watch as they have for centuries as we amble on, *sans* mules, simply an old dog and an old man, but to them mere youngsters.

We're on a double dirt mule track and saunter reverently on the horizontal stretch for a welcome change among the silent trees. If it's later in the year and early in the morning, the low sun, which from this altitude has risen a little above the coastal mountain range to the east, illuminates the scene in bursts of brilliant beams through the vegetation. It's magical. I promise you, if you are ever going to meet elves and fairies, it will be in such a place as this. It was here we had our first encounter with the Lord of the Kingdom of the Mountains.

I rely on my dog when we're out; his senses alert me to what's around us, as they did that morning. The ancient, gnarled olives are to our left as we walk, a plantation of younger almond trees to the right, at ground level overgrown with grasses and spiky gorse. On the path, Pascual is happily trotting along about three metres in front, occasionally looking round to check that the old man hasn't gone astray. The dog halts, ears up, nose up, tail at half-mast. An alarm bell has rung in his head. I stop in my tracks too and alter the grip on my stick, spinning it so its knobbly- knuckled heavy handle hangs down by my foot. You never can tell what might come rushing at you out of the bush so soon after sunrise.

I stand tense; the moment is electrifying; the time slows. Pascual lowers his shoulders; I lift mine and turn sideways towards where he's peering into the bushes. Unexpectedly, a creature crashes from the undergrowth—not the boar I expected, but a great big golden beast with huge turned-back horns.

It hadn't been aware of us until now. I see the white of his eye. Pascual barks and I nearly wet myself. The animal doesn't want to attack; he wants to get away and starts running towards the square of light where the track opens up at the end of the corridor of trees. Pascual, who weighs at most 23 kilos, a fifth if not less of the goat's bulk, runs behind in a pointless chase.

I go into fast adrenalin-powered-mode-walk, also in pursuit. I want to see what happens. The Golden Beauty takes off at speed. To the right, at the edge of the olive grove, is an ancient dry-stone wall. Things morph into slow motion, as, to my astonishment, with no effort, the wondrous creature lifts himself from the earth as though by some elevatory power and flies straight up the two-metre-high wall, landing on the other side, at a run on the stony ground between the trees. The move he made, a single sideways gravity-defying bound, astonished me! Then he was gone, disappeared into the bright morning light, leaving a big hole where he was a second ago.

Pascual couldn't match his leap. A couple of years back, it would have been no problem. Frustrated, he runs up and down, as I stand there trying to make sense of the preceding few seconds.

My first close encounter with a male *arruí* is now etched into my memory of extraordinary experiences.

It wasn't the last time we were to see him.

Some weeks later, further into the mellow times of autumn, we're on the same trail as usual. Pascual leads the way.

Near to where we had the previous adventure, the pathway reaches a junction. In front, there's low thorny scrub, gorse, and tangles of heather. It's an expanse of rugged, uncultivated land with a steep falling off the cliff edge and a panoramic vista of our neighbouring village far below and to a clear view of the coast beyond.

This is the point a visitor could stand to admire the shining towers of Benidorm. Instead, we turn right onto the rocky, dusty path skirting the top of the mountain. We amble along, drinking in the lovely autumn morning. It was precisely then that Pascual shot off! What was he after this time?

He left the trail and scooted down into the bush at a speed belying an old dog, then disappeared. You would think he was a pensioner on a double dose of steroids, late for a heavy date. Where'd he gone? I didn't worry too much; after all, he'd lived most of his life on a mountainside not far away. But something said, "Keep him in sight." During moments like these, you don't know if he's chasing boar, sheep, or an open tin of Spam on a window ledge. I soon found out.

Breathless, I stopped at what I saw below the path amongst the rocks and gorse. I felt I'd morphed into Sir David Attenborough. Below, about fifty metres away, was a herd of the goats, gleaming golden fleeces decked out on top with an armoury of curving horns. All of them turned, becoming a spiky wall focused on my daft old dog who was leading a solitary Charge of the Dogs Light Brigade towards them.

There were about thirty animals, females, little ones, younger males—and Himself, The Lord of the Kingdom of the Mountains, standing four-square as if he owned the place. Fearlessly, Pascual charged them. I'd thought he was about due for a centenary telegram from the Queen but at that moment he wasn't feeling his age. He saw creatures that needed sorting out. His instinct, being a shepherd dog, was to round them up and read them the riot act.

Standing stock-still and on full alert, I remained rooted to the spot, impotent, a witness; the only human watching a great drama unfolding as my brave, crazy old dog flew over rocks, burst through bushes and spiky grasses; he was shepherding again, with a job to do! I felt helpless, like a dad on the edge of the playing field, as his son gets beaten up in the scrum. Would Pascual get beaten up—or worse?

The males, bristling with their large pointy horns, were on to him and stood together in defence. The ewes and younger ones became alarmed and scattered to the safety of the precipice behind them. To these extraordinary animals, a sheer rock cliff is nothing; but to Pascual, it might come as a bit of a shock.

To my surprise and astonishment, the nerve of most of the young males caved in and they split too, in all directions, including Him! Pascual, the brown bullet, didn't miss a beat and disappeared into the bush after them. Then everything went quiet, and the world paused in its tracks.

All silent; he'd gone, they'd gone. There was a cliff behind them. In my mind's eye, I saw Pascual, in slow-motion, not realising it was there, he off the edge, the goats all watching and giggling on the rock wall, as he floundered in space falling a thousand feet to an inglorious death. My poor DOG!

I stayed where I was; I had no idea what to do. Should I call the wife, or Steve my pal in England? He is a practical sort of chap; he'd think of something. Should I try to follow—and do what? My inner voice, as though it knew, said *Stay there*.

Pascual was after the entire herd, the nutter. What if he did it? What if he came trotting back, pleased as punch, with twenty wild beasts in front of him? What if he brought them home? What would I say to Kath? "I've been looking for alternative accommodation for them darling, honest." Where would we put them? It's a small house with antique rugs!

So, there I am, dog over the cliff, future uncertain, thinking of a name for the new puppy, when the bushes shook about fifty metres away.

I looked; what was that? It was Pascual, a wild-eyed demented creature escaping the revenge of hell, running as fast as he could go in such a rough landscape. Then I realised he was looking straight at me, and if he could, he'd be screaming DAAAAAAAD HELP!!!!

Not surprising, as the whole Wild Goat Nation (Alicante Region Association) was after him, about ten metres behind, smashing through the undergrowth. Out in front, The Lord of the Mountains, never mind the Spanish Bull. The last thing you want is a great big one with ribbed needle-sharp horns up you!

It was obvious the hunter had become the hunted, and he knew it. He was running for his life as fast as his old legs could carry him. Chasing him was the beast, hackles raised, and Pascual was coming straight towards *me*! He had bitten off far more than he could chew, and Himself the Magnificent was intent on teaching him a lesson, maiming or killing him with those horns and trampling him beneath those hooves, as the ladies and younger males watched.

The pursuer was on my dog. At one point, it reached him and butted him on his flank, almost knocking him off balance in his flight, but he stayed upright. Come on boy, COME ON!

They were getting closer by the second; Himself looking all powerful and pissed off big time, following Pascual and heading straight for me!

Pascual was making for sanctuary. I was about twenty metres away. Would he make it? Will his heart give out? The big bull, horns down close behind. Then a little voice spoke up. I think he was a staff-member in my Life Preservation Department.

"Sorry to disturb you, sir, but have you noticed?" the voice said politely.

"What?"

"They're coming right at you, sir."

Bloody hell, they were. I had a reward treat in my pocket for Pascual, but not for half a tonne of mountain anger and muscle with skewers on top.

Pascual remained upright while nimbly dodging and weaving about the sharp rocks and spiky vegetation. Close on his tail trailing clouds of adrenalin, came the Him.

"Don't you think you should do something?" suggested the voice a bit timidly. "They're almost upon you, sir."

"YAAAAAAGGGGHHHHH!" I screamed at the top of my old Yorkshire lungs and from the bottom of my animal being with all the volume I could muster. I raised my arms and jabbed my walking stick in the air and shook it about like a small tree, holding my pose, jacket blowing in the wind, trying to look as big as I could. He would have to reckon with me. I remember thinking how relieved I was at that moment that I had my most butch beanie hat on!

The scene changed from carnage on the hoof to cartoon in an instant, as the Him screeched to a halt (I kid you not, apart from the screech) and stared at the strange dark creature above him on the hill, in silhouette with the sun behind me. The Great Lord of the Mountains, not even breathless, had done enough. To my absolute astonishment, he turned slowly and deliberately, walking away with his few young males in support through the bushes where, as I watched, the rest of the herd greeted him. Honour served and all safe, they calmly disappeared back into their world.

Pascual made it to my side. Me—I was in a state of shaking shock and leaning on my stick. I looked down at the dog. He was panting. We both realised the other was okay.

I rubbed Pascual's head. "Phew, my God. I don't know. Come on, let's rest a minute." He nodded in support. "Do not do that again, please!" I swear he smiled. I gave him a treat.

We sat there as the sun climbed a little higher into that silent, perfect morning. He looked at me; I looked at him. I put my arm around his neck, and pulled him towards me, feeling his age and mine, and laughed out loud for both of us and life.

"You nearly got yourself killed, you silly old bugger."

He didn't care. He was here, safe, with me, together, in the moment. Every fibre of his old body was alive. All he wanted was another treat.

Epilogue

Six years after I wrote the last story of this book, on 23 November 2023 Pascualet, the last shepherd's dog, passed away peacefully at home at 15 years and three months of age, surrounded by family and friends.

He had spent the first eight years of his life on a steep and rocky mountainside keeping goats and sheep in order. By the time he reached fourteen, his amazing sure-footedness and strength had waned. In the autumn of this year, our house, rather than his sanctuary, had become more of an obstacle course without the fun.

He was going deaf and blind, struggling to stand, sit, or walk. In a three-storey house, he faced daily challenges, often tumbling down the stairs to the dining room or stumbling on the way up to the lounge. He had so many falls it's a wonder he wasn't just a skinful of broken bones. He could no longer navigate the metal spiral staircase leading to the mezzanine and garden below the terrace. Instead, he would stand on the top landing staring down, desperate to be with me while I worked on my walking sticks or watered the plants.

Eventually, we had to stay behind him going up the stairs and in front of him going down in case he missed his step. The day that happened, it was clear that the time had come.

For me, never mind his incontinence, deafness, and onset of dementia, when he couldn't climb the stairs anymore, our house became his prison and we the unwitting warders.

For many owners of older dogs, the decision to euthanise them is difficult. I mean, just that morning, hadn't he looked so young again, didn't he have that old spark in his amber eyes, and wasn't he sprightly on his short walk? Shouldn't we give him a few more weeks and us a little more time to share with the creature who had entered our new life in Spain and changed it?

He was a dog who had touched many human lives, villagers and expats alike. Everyone knew him. His reputation was legendary. When we took him on, the locals wagged their heads; they expected us to fail. Pascualet would not be penned. It astonished them when we quietened, but didn't break, our little Lion. Now, however, the animal that changed our lives had reached the end of his.

The day and the hour arrived. Promptly at two in the afternoon, the vet appeared, her leather bag in hand. Kath and I were sombre and apprehensive, doing our best to maintain some composure. Pascual, who didn't even bark at the newcomer, stayed on his dog bed, accepting the strangeness of the circumstance. Besides the vet, two other people, who meant a lot to him, were present at his earthly end. A senior lady, Clara, to whom Pascual was a link to her past with Salvador, and a man in his mid-seventies, Michael, to whom he'd been a constant friend and regular visitor when he ran loose and wild in the mountains. They were there to say goodbye.

His passing was calm and quick. Human eyes brimmed with tears as Michael stroked his back and I held his paw. Then he was gone and bundled up in his dog bed.

Michael and his wife, Christine, have a wonderful house nearby, overlooking a grand valley surrounded by mountains. It's a place where they spoiled Pascual with treats from their table, where he loved to run, jump, and hunt for wild rabbits. They had offered to have him buried there under an old olive tree. That's what we did that day. It's where he's at rest today. We can visit any time they said. Right now, as we complete this book, the daffodils that Christine planted are flowering upon his grave.

In the first days after his passing, Kath and I were emotional zombies. He had been a daily part of our lives for eight years, but now there was an empty space.

He's still there in that space. We feel his presence in different ways. Because of his dementia, he had a habit of standing motionless in the middle of a room and constantly wandering in and out of the kitchen terrace doorway. Kath had to open the door slowly to avoid hitting his head, as he might be standing in front of it outside in the dark, waiting to come in. She still opens the door, anticipating him being there.

For me, without him and without our regular five-kilometre walk, which was a cherished part of my day, I was left feeling lonely and vulnerable in the mountains and countryside.

After a couple of weeks, I resumed our walks and realised that so much of my experience was his experience. His every move and reaction, when his senses were full on, felt like an extension of my own. I watched him as much as I watched the rocky path and the surrounding wild terrain. We grew so very close. When I'm out now, the landscape is not the same book I read through my dog's reactions. As an old man, I walk cautiously, mindful of my steps. I whistle and cough and bang on rocks with my stick, announcing my presence to the wild boar whose territory I am passing through. His absence has forever changed the *campo* for me.

I dedicate this book to our much-loved Pascualet—companion, guard, guide, and intermediary between us and the local people of our village. He's gone, but in the campo his spirit lives on, as does his legacy in the memories of many.

Acknowledgements

I want to give a special thanks for a group of landlords in New York City. Thanks for being so single-minded that you forced my wife to leave her businesses in your properties. It was meant to be. We left the Big Apple forever, landing in a magical location far, far away where life has been very good. We didn't know it at the time, but you did us a huge favour. And no, you can't charge us for it.

I would like to thank my Beta Readers who gave immensely useful feedback with the speed of lightening. They are Gilliam Anderson, Patrick Argent, Michael Forkin, Maggie Gibbs, Nicki Glasser, Kurt Gualtieri, Katherine Henderson, Joe and Laura Medred, Veronica Moore, Juan F. Ripoll, Stephen Shaw, Laura Sunderland, Christopher Webster, and Sue Wilkinson. In combination, they provided all sorts of insights, corrections, and guidance that helped bring the book to fruition.

A special thanks to my editor Brenda Gilbert. She brought me down to earth as many times as I floated up and off it.

A great big thank you to Robin Phillips of Author Help for his steadfast patience and professionalism while getting us through the final publishing stages.

Thanks to all the good people of Tàrbena, named and not, who provided inspiration for my stories and continue to do so.

I especially want to thank my wife for making this book happen. The experience was as challenging as it was rewarding. She never lost the vision, never gave up. From when we first met, collaborating on writing projects with her over the dining room table has been such a joy in my life.

And a big fat thanks to Pascual, bless his soul. He introduced me to the wonders beyond the village, into the big wide-open *campo*, his natural, wild world with all its mysteries, adventures, and truths.

I never had a better hiking buddy.

Thank you for reading *The Last Shepherd's Dog*. I sincerely hope you enjoyed reading it as much as I enjoyed writing it. If you did…

1. Contact me and join my mailing list at www.johnsunderland.co.uk/contact
2. Come like my Facebook page https://www.facebook.com/johnsunderlandwrites/
3. Visit my website https://johnsunderland.co.uk/
4. Help other people find this book by writing a review. I would be very grateful if you could spend just five minutes leaving a review (it can be as short as you like) on the book's Amazon page or your favourite reading site.

About The Last Shepherd's Dog

In 2017, John and Kathy escaped New York City to experience authentic Spanish village life in Tàrbena, Spain. John began posting narratives on Facebook called *Tàrbena Times*, inspired by his experiences in and around their village, mostly hilarious, sometimes moving and often surreal. He and Kathy chose the best ones, polished several up and collected them in this first of a series of stories called *The Last Shepherd's Dog and Other Stories from a Rural Spanish Village High and Hidden in the Costa Blanca Mountains*.

About the Author

John Sunderland is the author of *On My Way to Jorvik: A humorous memoir of how a boy with a vision became a radical designer, created Dusty Bin, made films with Kenny Everett then revolutionised visitor attraction design forever.* You can find his books on Amazon, online, and at your favourite book seller or go to https://johnsunderland.co.uk and click on the "Get the Book" link.

John is a born and bred North Yorkshireman. He started his career at age 11 as a truant from maths at QEGS in Wakefield, UK. Hiding in the museum, art gallery and cinema, he wished museums could be more like films. He became a freelance designer, filmmaker and animator and created the iconic cartoon mascot Dusty Bin for Yorkshire TV's popular 3*2*1 game show. In 1981 he became Project Designer of the original Jorvik Viking Centre in York, UK making a museum more like a film. From there he built 24 commercially successful and award-winning international museums and cultural heritage centres. John maintained journals of his design journey. One hundred and sixty of them are now housed at the Borthwick Institute for Archives, University of York, York, United Kingdom.

Kathy Kirkpatrick, his wife, was co-founder and owner of Life Café in the East Village of New York city from 1982 until 2012. The café was featured in the Broadway musical hit, RENT by Jonathan Larson, one of her regular customers.

John and Kathy currently live in the village of Tàrbena in the Costa Blanca Mountains of Spain. John paints, writes, and carves walking sticks out of wood pruned and collected from the local groves as he walks his adopted dog Pascual, who once belonged to the last shepherd of the village. In between sticks, he writes, illustrates books, paints, and adds daily to his 40-year collection of journals.

www.ingramcontent.com/pod-product-compliance
Lightning Source LLC
Chambersburg PA
CBHW020519080526
44583CB00013B/662